"*Echoes of Eden* is the most accessible, readable, and yet theologically robust work on Christianity and the arts that you will be able to find. It is biblical, theologically sound, filled with examples, and edifying. It anticipates and answers well all the most common questions that evangelical people ask about the arts. I highly recommend it."

    Tim Keller, Pastor, Redeemer Presbyterian Church, New York City; author, *The Reason for God*

"Jerram Barrs clearly loves the Christian vision of being human, and he loves human beings of all sorts. In this book he helps us to enjoy the fundamentally human activity of the arts, showing us how 'all great art contains elements of the true story: the story of the good creation, the fallen world, and the longing for redemption.' The chapters giving us a tour of great Christian writers—Lewis, Tolkien, Rowling, Shakespeare, and Austen—bubble over with passionate delight in these authors' artistic and moral achievements."

    C. John Collins, Professor of Old Testament, Covenant Theological Seminary; author, *Did Adam and Eve Really Exist?*

"A beautiful book on the contours of beauty by a beautiful man. Jerram Barrs here presents a lifetime of meditations on a subject close to his heart. The arts, he argues, are not a luxury, nor are they the savior. Instead they are an integral part of human life because they provide a unique window onto divine truth and the truth of the divine. The chapter on how to judge the arts is alone worth the price of admission. Reading these pages one can tell that art is not the *subject* for Jerram, but a rich palette, one he has lived with over the years. The arts, in his assessment, tell us not only what has been lost after Eden, but also how we may return to that gorgeous land. This book will enrich both professional artists and anyone else sensitive to the power of the arts for all of life."

    William Edgar, Professor of Apologetics, Westminster Theological Seminary, Philadelphia; author, *Schaeffer on the Christian Life*

"One of the obvious virtues of this book is its balance between theory and literary criticism of specific authors. The first five chapters are a carefully constructed Christian aesthetic. The second half of the book applies the theory to five authors. The splendid organization of the book makes it easy to read, and there is an admirable range in the subjects covered, as the five theoretic chapters systematically discuss the questions that Christians really ask about the arts, while the addition of Shakespeare and Jane Austen to Christian fantasy writers provides a pleasing scope. Finally, the book has a latent apologetic angle that I liked, not only in the theoretic chapters with their defense of the arts, but also in the chapters on specific authors, as Barrs explains why he is an enthusiast for each of them."

Leland Ryken, Professor of English, Wheaton College

"This is a wonderful book, especially for those who want to enhance their knowledge of how the church should view the arts. Jerram Barrs brings an intellectually informed and profoundly pastoral approach to confront the misunderstanding and animosity that frequently exist between evangelical Christians and popular contemporary literature such as the Harry Potter series. This book is a must read for anyone who has a burden to see the creation as it is reflected in today's pop culture."

Mike Higgins, Dean of Students, Covenant Theological Seminary

"Jerram Barrs offers a compelling Christian defense of the imagination as a vehicle of truth and of the need to reclaim an imitative (as opposed to a self-expressive) view of the arts. He not only quotes C. S. Lewis wisely, but has written a book of which Lewis would have approved."

Louis Markos, Professor in English, Scholar in Residence, and Robert H. Ray Chair in Humanities, Houston Baptist University; author, *Restoring Beauty: The Good, the True, and the Beautiful in the Writings of C. S. Lewis*

"For as long as I have known him, Jerram Barrs has passionately loved the arts. In *Echoes of Eden* he lets us share his passion by allowing us a glimpse of the beauty, truth, and grace he sees in the imaginative work of C. S. Lewis, J. R. R. Tolkien, J. K. Rowling, William Shakespeare, and Jane Austen. If he stopped there, this would be a book worth reading, but he digs far deeper, framing our understanding of the arts within the biblical worldview. From that perspective, human creativity is a good gift of God in a broken world, an expression of the image of the Creator in which we are made. Because of the brokenness, Barrs outlines eleven broad categories by which to judge a piece of art, since God's image is always portrayed in ways that are flawed and incomplete. I hope *Echoes of Eden* is read and discussed widely by Christians. The truth of its message can help nurture a Christian imagination, restore the arts to their proper place in the church, and help us frame the unchanging gospel in a way that will cause a postmodern world to consider its claims."

Denis D. Haack, Director, Ransom Fellowship; Visiting Instructor, Covenant Theological Seminary

"This is a marvelous book for Christians who wish to think well and biblically about culture. Professor Barrs's thesis—that human cultural production always has its genesis in something I have for years called the 'Edenic memory'—is spot-on. By providing a careful theological analysis of the origins of culture, the book teaches us how to live wisely and rightly in a world overflowing with cultural artifacts. Barrs's observation on the nature and role of fantasy in the Harry Potter chapter is particularly thoughtful, and his chapter on how we are to judge the arts is as fine as anything I've read on the subject."

Grant Horner, Associate Professor of Renaissance and Reformation, The Master's College; author, *Meaning at the Movies*

"Evangelical Christianity has long been conflicted over the arts and in particular the literary artistry of such lights as Austen, Tolkien, and Rowling. Some justify such literature only insofar as it functions as an elaborately coded gospel tract. Others, despairing of any Christian rationale, confess such writings to be a distraction, a guilty pleasure, or even satanic. Now, with his typical blend of profundity and lucidity, Jerram Barrs clears away the clutter of much-touted but ultimately muddled arguments and sets forth a clear framework for any Christians interested in thinking biblically about art, not least those Christians who like to spend time in such places as Hogwarts or Middle-earth. Turn the page and prepare to worship!"

Nicholas Perrin, Dean, Wheaton College Graduate School

"In a clear and attractive style, Jerram Barrs writes with passion about the 'echoes of Eden' in the arts, which are so central to our humanity, whatever our beliefs. Graciously and with wisdom, he picks up a conversation that has already included such Christian thinkers as John Calvin, Dorothy L. Sayers, J. R. R. Tolkien, and C. S. Lewis. Illustrations that he draws from the fiction of Lewis, Tolkien, J. K. Rowling, the still enormously popular Jane Austen, and others make even more vivid his insightful reflections. Reading his gift of a book is an enriching and inspiring experience not to be missed."

Colin Duriez, author, *J. R. R. Tolkien: The Making of a Legend* and *C. S. Lewis: A Biography of Friendship*

"When a lawyer asked Jesus, 'Who is my neighbor?' Jesus didn't preach a sermon; he told a story, and with it he disclosed a profound truth. In *Echoes of Eden*, Jerram Barrs shows us how novelists, playwrights, and poets—much like Jesus—open our eyes and broaden our understanding. He shows us how, by creating worlds, people, problems, and circumstances, great writers put us in touch with the human condition: the struggles and joys, as well as the grief and great satisfactions. In these few pages, Barrs shows us why, especially in the twenty-first century, we need good books: they help us become fully human."

Richard Doster, Editor, *byFaith* magazine; author, *Safe at Home*

Other Crossway Books by Jerram Barrs

Learning Evangelism from Jesus

The Heart of Evangelism

Through His Eyes: God's Perspective on Women in the Bible

Echoes of
EDEN

Reflections *on* Christianity, Literature, *and the* Arts

JERRAM BARRS

CROSSWAY

WHEATON, ILLINOIS

Trade paperback ISBN: 978-1-4335-3597-0
Mobipocket ISBN: 978-1-4335-3599-4
PDF ISBN: 978-1-4335-3598-7
ePub ISBN: 978-1-4335-3600-7

Library of Congress Cataloging-in-Publication Data
Barrs, Jerram.
    Echoes of Eden : reflections on Christianity, literature, and the arts / Jerram Barrs.
        pages cm
    Includes bibliographical references and index.
        ISBN 978-1-4335-3597-0 (tp)
1. Christianity and the arts. I. Title.
BR115.A8B375   2013
261.5'7—dc23   2012050928

Crossway is a publishing ministry of Good News Publishers.

VP		25	24	23	22	21	20	19	18	17	16	15	14	13
15	14	13	12	11	10	9	8	7	6	5	4	3	2	1

To my beloved wife, Vicki,
who has been for me the primary
inspiration for *Echoes of Eden*,
by her constant love and encouragement
in all my writing and teaching,
and above all by her commitment and devotion,
which has been for forty-five years
a daily reminder of Eden
and of God's happy design
for married life

"A wife of noble character
who can find?
She is worth far more
than rubies." (NIV)

"Many women
have done excellently,
but you
surpass them all."

Contents

1 God and Humans as Creative Artists ... 11

2 Imitation, the Heart of the Christian's Approach to Creativity ... 23

3 Building a Christian Understanding of the Artist's Calling ... 39

4 How Do We Judge the Arts? ... 53

5 Echoes of Eden: God's Testimony to the Truth ... 67

6 The Conversion of C. S. Lewis and Echoes of Eden in His Life ... 85

7 Echoes of Eden in Tolkien's *Lord of the Rings* ... 105

8 Harry Potter and the Triumph of Self-Sacrificing Love ... 125

9 Shakespeare and a Christian Worldview ... 147

10 Jane Austen, Novelist of the Human Heart ... 169

Appendix: The "Outing" of Dumbledore ... 193

General Index ... 195

Scripture Index ... 203

1

God and Humans as Creative Artists

Thinking scripturally about the arts is an area where there appears to be great confusion in our churches. On the one hand, many Christians have been taught that, as believers in Christ, we ought only to listen to music, read books, or watch films that have been produced by fellow believers. On the other hand, almost all Christians will, in fact, read newspapers and books, watch television shows and movies, go to plays and musicals, listen to music, and buy art cards and pictures for our walls simply because we *like* these things. And we will do this without much reflection on who produced them, unless we encounter something that is obviously blasphemous, gratuitously violent, or clearly pornographic.

Even those who suggest most passionately that Christians should only enjoy art by other Christians will take delight in buildings, bridges, roads, interior decoration, clothes, or beautifully prepared and presented meals, and they will take this delight without asking whether the architect, builder, designer, manufacturer, or chef is a committed believer in the Lord Jesus Christ.

So, how are Christians to think about the arts? To approach this subject, we begin with the biblical doctrine of creation.

God, the Creator of All Things, Visible and Invisible

Every orthodox creed and every believing theologian throughout the history of the church has affirmed the Christian's faith in God, the Creator of heaven and earth and of all things visible and invisible. We all have our favorite scriptural passages that affirm this doctrine, that express our hope in the Lord who made all things, and that communicate this faith and hope with words of marvelous beauty. Two such passages are Psalm 8:1,

> O LORD, our Lord,
>> how majestic is your name in all the earth!

and Psalm 19:1,

> The heavens declare the glory of God,
>> and the sky above proclaims his handiwork.

We praise God now for the wonder of his creation, and we will praise him for this for all eternity:

> Worthy are you, our Lord and God,
>> to receive glory and honor and power,
> for you created all things,
>> and by your will they existed and were created. (Rev. 4:11)

Many other Scriptures also explore this conviction—sometimes at great length, as well as in glorious poetry; see, for instance, Job 38–41, Psalm 148, and Psalm 19 (a psalm that C. S. Lewis called one of the greatest lyric poems ever written).

John Calvin, in exquisitely beautiful French prose, writes of the wonder of God's creation in words that retain their remarkable power even in our English translations and are worth quoting at length:

> 1. Since the perfection of blessedness consists in the knowledge of God, he has been pleased, in order that none might be excluded from the means of obtaining felicity, not only to deposit in our minds that seed of religion of which we have already spoken, but so to manifest his perfections in the whole structure of the universe, and daily place himself in our view, that we cannot open our eyes without being compelled to behold him. His essence, indeed, is incomprehensible, utterly transcending all human thought; but on each of his works his glory is engraven in characters so bright, so distinct, and so illustrious, that none, however

dull and illiterate, can plead ignorance as their excuse. . . . And because the glory of his power and wisdom is more refulgent in the firmament, it is frequently designated as his palace. And, first, wherever you turn your eyes, there is no portion of the world, however minute, that does not exhibit at least some sparks of beauty; while it is impossible to contemplate the vast and beautiful fabric as it extends around, without being overwhelmed by the immense weight of glory. Hence, the author of the Epistle to the Hebrews elegantly describes the visible worlds as images of the invisible (Heb. 11:3), the elegant structure of the world serving us as a kind of mirror, in which we may behold God, though otherwise invisible. . . .

2. In attestation of his wondrous wisdom, both the heavens and the earth present us with innumerable proofs, not only those more recondite proofs which astronomy, medicine, and all the natural sciences are designed to illustrate, but proofs which force themselves on the notice of the most illiterate peasant, who cannot open his eyes without beholding them. It is true, indeed, that those who are more or less intimately acquainted with those liberal studies are thereby assisted and enabled to obtain a deeper insight into the secret workings of divine wisdom. No man, however, though he be ignorant of these, is incapacitated for discerning such proofs of creative wisdom as may well cause him to break forth in admiration of the Creator. . . . Still, none who have the use of their eyes can be ignorant of the divine skill manifested so conspicuously in the endless variety, yet distinct and well-ordered array, of the heavenly host; and, therefore it is plain that the Lord has furnished every man with abundant proofs of his wisdom.[1]

The English poet Gerard Manley Hopkins delights us with his poetic paean of praise in one of his best-known works, "God's Grandeur":

The world is charged with the grandeur of God.
   It will flame out, like shining from shook foil.

---

[1]John Calvin, *Institutes of the Christian Religion*, trans. Henry Beveridge, rev. ed. (Peabody, MA: Hendrickson, 2008), 1.5.1–2.

In another of Hopkins's poems, "Pied Beauty," we find that he holds up for our pleasure the amazing diversity of color, texture, taste, and action in creation:

> Glory be to God for dappled things—
>> For skies of couple-colour as a brinded cow;
>>> For rose-moles all in stipple upon trout that swim;
>> Fresh-firecoal chestnut falls; finches' wings;
>>> Landscape plotted and pieced—fold, fallow, and plough;
>>> And áll trádes, their gear and tackle and trim.
>
> All things counter, original, spare, strange;
>> Whatever is fickle, freckled (who knows how?)
>>> With swift, slow; sweet, sour; adazzle, dim;
>> He fathers-forth whose beauty is past change:
>>> Praise him.

Daniel Loizeaux considers God's creativity under four headings. He writes: "How God's imagination daily loads us with benefits. Contemplate this embarrassment of riches from a four-fold aspect: their perfection, diversity, profusion, inventiveness."[2] I am indebted to Loizeaux's discussion in my own exploration of these four aspects of God's creative genius.

Perfection

If we look under a microscope at anything God has made to see it in all its detail, we will discover that the more we see, the more amazing is his creative genius. A closer view enables us to see new and unimagined beauties and infinitesimally tiny wonders. Look at the structure of a leaf, a diamond, a snowflake, or a human cell. If we compare any product of human technology to any work of God—for example, try looking at an object made of polished steel, copper, or bronze—and try the same experiment in magnification, we very soon will observe the difference. What God has made is

---

[2] Daniel Loizeaux, "The Imagination of God," *Genesis: Journal of the Society of Christians in the Arts, Inc.* 1, no. 2 (1975): 72.

lovely to our eyes, but our own works, viewed under a microscope, show their flaws.

Diversity

Think of the many different varieties of birds, insects, trees, and flowers; or for an even more extraordinary example, the infinite variety of snowflakes, sunrises, sunsets, or—more importantly—human beings: no two are exactly the same.

Several times over the past few years my wife and I have traveled to Naples, a city on the Gulf Coast of Florida, to stay for a few weeks in a friend's home just five minutes' walk from the beach. Each afternoon when we are there we join the many other people who return to the beach to watch the sun go down over the Gulf—each day it is glorious, and each day it is different. In each moment of each sunset there is constant change, and yet every moment has its own glory and perfect beauty.

Profusion

God loves abundance: think of those daily sunsets or the flowers in a meadow, or the stars in the night sky—if you can get away from bright city lights to see them, such as out in a deep forest, in a desert, or high up on a mountain. In such a setting, the sky seems to be nothing but stars. Indeed, astronomers tell us that there are sixty billion galaxies in the universe, and that each one of these galaxies contains between ten billion and a hundred billion stars. Our sun is just one of these untold billions of stars. Such profusion is unimaginable to us.

I remember going hiking in the Sierra Mountains in Central California with my sons and a friend and his family. We slept out in the open, and one night we set out our sleeping bags by the shore of a small lake at about eleven thousand feet. It was a clear night and we lay there looking up at the stars. The number of them and the brightness of their light overwhelmed us. Then the moon rose over the mountains across the lake, and I burst out with the words of Psalm 8:

O Lord, our Lord,
> how majestic is your name in all the earth!
You have set your glory above the heavens. . . .

When I look at the heavens, the work of your fingers,
> the moon and stars, which you have set in place . . . (vv. 1–3)

Then, together we sang hymns and songs of praise. We had to express something of our awe and wonder at the loveliness of this world and of the glory of its Maker.

Inventiveness

We admire men and women who come up with new designs, and rightly so. But just think how this activity is only an infinitesimally tiny copy of the inventiveness of the Lord, who delights in making all things new—not just at the beginning of the creation, but every day.

Not Asceticism but the Glad Reception and Enjoyment of the Gifts of God's Creativity

It is evident as we read Genesis 1 that God believed that all he had made was good. Repeatedly during the account of the creation, this refrain occurs: "God saw that it ["the light," v. 4] was good" (Gen. 1:4, 10, 12, 18, 21, 25). At the literary high point of the text, when we read that he had created man, we find this expression of the Lord's delight in his work: "And God saw everything that he had made, and behold, it was very good" (1:31).

However, some Christians believe that this world and the created order are no longer good after the fall. One writer puts it this way: "Before the Fall there was an earth; now there is a world; after the Second Coming there will be a kingdom." He goes on to say that everything of this old creation—even inanimate matter—is contaminated by the spirit of antichrist, indwelt by the Devil, and under the power of darkness. The writer concludes, therefore, that the enjoyment of life and of God's daily gifts is no longer genuinely spiritual; for such enjoyment is tainted with carnality and therefore in some manner suspect and inherently dangerous to us.

Calvin responded to such a view with a resounding affirmation of the beauty of this world and the appropriateness of delight in God's creation gifts: "Should the Lord have attracted our eyes to the beauty of the flowers, and our sense of smell to pleasant odors, and should it then be sin to drink them in? Has he not even made the colors so that the one is more wonderful than the other?"[3]

Scripture itself insists not only that delight in creation and the enjoyment of God's gifts are right and good, but also that asceticism—the claim that taking pleasure in our creaturely life is somehow unspiritual or even sinful—is in fact a heretical teaching. If heresy seems an excessive charge, then consider Paul's passionate words in 1 Timothy 4:1–5, an example of a biblical denunciation of the teaching that it is ungodly to enjoy the gifts of life:

> Now the Spirit expressly says that in later times some will depart from the faith by devoting themselves to deceitful spirits and teachings of demons, through the insincerity of liars whose consciences are seared, who forbid marriage and require abstinence from foods that God created to be received with thanksgiving by those who believe and know the truth. For everything created by God is good, and nothing is to be rejected if it is received with thanksgiving, for it is made holy by the word of God and prayer.

In these words, Paul insists that food, sex, marriage—indeed all the gifts of creation—are good and holy, for God himself has declared them to be so in his Word. Paul demands that we see that asceticism, even if it comes under the guise of spirituality, is heretical, even demonic. Why does he speak with such impassioned language? The simple answer is that the teaching that it is sinful to enjoy the gifts of creation is deeply blasphemous because it is a rejection of God's own valuation of creation. Asceticism turns its back on God and regards his creation as worthless, or even worse, as somehow corrupting to us, as if creation itself were a source of sin.

---

[3]John Calvin, *On the Life of the Christian Man* (Grand Rapids: Baker, 1952), 88.

Repeatedly in the history of the church, Christians have been tempted to devalue the richness of creation—and therefore the arts—as if it would be somehow more "spiritual" to live a life devoid of beauty, of good things, of music, of literature, of painting, of color, and so forth. It is as if bare simplicity, barrenness, and even ugliness were somehow more pleasing to God. Behind this idea is the conviction that the "spiritual" is all that matters, and that the physical, therefore, is at best only of secondary value. In this view, the arts are considered optional, rather extravagant, an unnecessary extra in life. But this belief is nonsense and, according to Paul, a heresy of the most serious kind, for in the end it is a denial of the goodness of creation and the goodness of its Creator.

The English poet and pastor George Herbert, in his poem "The Elixir," captured this obligation of the Christian to value as good all that God has made. This poem may be found in many hymnals; I include here stanzas 1, 4, and 6:

Teach me, my God and King,
  In all things thee to see,
And what I do in anything
  To do it as for thee.

All may of thee partake:
  Nothing can be so mean
Which with his tincture, "for thy sake,"
  Will not grow bright and clean.

This is the famous stone
  That turneth all to gold;
For that which God doth touch and own
  Cannot for lesse be told.

Reflecting further on this theme, we may point to five foundational doctrines that affirm the value of the richness of life here in this world:

- *Creation.* See, again, Genesis 1 with its repeated "God saw that it was good" and Paul's words in 1 Timothy 4:1–5 (quoted above). God commands us to agree with him, to acknowledge that everything that he has made is good, and then to receive this good work of his with thankful and glad hearts.
- *Common grace, or God's providential care for all creation.* See Genesis 9:8–17 and the everlasting covenant that God makes with all creatures after the flood. God cares for *all* creation, as evidenced in Psalms 104 and 145, and also in Jesus's words in Matthew 6:26–29 and 10:29–31, where he speaks of God watching over and providing for the flowers and the birds and, even more, all people.
- *The incarnation.* The eternal Son of God, the second person of the Trinity, became flesh; he became a man; he became a part of this universe—not merely for the thirty-three years of his earthly life, but for all eternity to come. Who can imagine a more remarkable affirmation of the physical than this, that the everlasting God who alone has immortality entered our world, joined the human race, and shares our life forever!
- *Bodily resurrection.* See Paul's joyful words about our physical resurrection in 1 Corinthians 15 and 2 Corinthians 5:1–5. Nothing expresses with greater clarity that our physical life in this world is precious than this conviction of God's commitment, "not that we would be unclothed, but that we would be further clothed, so that what is mortal may be swallowed up by life" (2 Cor. 5:4).
- *The new creation.* There will be a renewed earth, with the curse removed (see Rom. 8:18–25; 2 Pet. 3:13; Rev. 21:1–4). This promise of the glory of the earth to come underlines the significance and value of all that God has made for our enjoyment here and now. Redemption will not be complete until our human life is restored to its full delight in the wonder of God's good creation.

God's Image Bearers as Sub-Creators

Man and woman, God's image bearers, are made to be sub-creators following after their Creator. The God who made all things made us to exercise dominion under him over this good creation (Gen. 1:26–28). In Psalm 8, David declares that this likeness to God, demonstrated as we rule over this earth and its creatures, constitutes our glory as human persons. He asks a question that many people ask when they are overwhelmed by the glory of creation (just as we were that night in the High Sierras):

> When I look at your heavens, the work of your fingers,
>   the moon and the stars, which you have set in place,
> what is man that you are mindful of him? (vv. 3–4)

David replies to his own question:

> You have made him a little lower than the heavenly beings
>   and crowned him with glory and honor.
> You have given him dominion over the works of your hands;
>   you have put all things under his feet. (vv. 5–6)

This answer by David challenges us never to devalue human beings, for we are crowned with the glory and honor of being like God. The universe in which we live may indeed be so remarkable and wonderful to us that we sometimes feel very small and insignificant when we look at its beauty or grandeur. But in Psalm 8 David teaches us that God's glory shines more brightly in each human person than it ever does in the loveliest night sky, the grandest mountain range, or the vastest ocean.

We are persons made to be like the personal God who made us and everything else around us. As those created to image God, we are designed by him to exercise rule over the creation in which we are set. In exercising dominion over God's good creation, we are not creators in an absolute sense, like God, but, rather, sub-creators at best. We never create *ex nihilo* (out of nothing) like God, for we are always working with some aspect of what he has already made. We might say that our dominion over this earth means that we "till the garden" of color, words, form and texture, sound and harmony, stone and clay, and imagination; of God's works in creation and of human works in history and in society. Sir Isaac

Newton likened our ruling the earth with the arts and sciences to the playing of a child: "I do not know what I may appear to the world; but to myself I seem to have been only like a boy, playing on the sea-shore, and diverting myself in now and then finding a smoother pebble or a prettier shell than ordinary, whilst the great ocean of truth lay all undiscovered before me."[4]

C. S. Lewis recognized that all great artists acknowledge that there is something outside themselves that is greater than they are, and that is greater than the works that they make: "The greatest poems (*indeed all of the greatest artistic works*) have been made by men who valued something else much more than poetry."[5] For the Christian, there needs to be a humble bowing before God the Creator and a glad acceptance of the gift of his created order with which we all do our work.

We exercise dominion now by "making things" with our hands, minds, and imaginations. This task will be ours forever, for on the renewed earth all the creative glory of all the nations will be brought into the kingdom of God to honor Christ (Rev. 21:24–26). Year by year we will go up from every part of this earth and bring what we have made to offer at the feet of Christ the King.

Sometimes Christians will insist that the only work that is truly worthwhile, pleasing to God, and spiritual is the work of serving the proclamation of the gospel across the world. This view suggests that if we were all truly earnest Christians, we would leave our "secular" jobs, in which we are simply making a living, providing for our families, and ruling the world, and we would all join the "sacred" work of mission. But if we stop and think about Jesus's life, we see that he was doing so-called secular work as a carpenter or a fisherman for many more years than he was a preacher and teacher. It would be blasphemous to suppose that during these years Jesus was living in a manner that was not fully godly and completely pleasing to his Father in heaven.

---

[4]Quoted in L. T. More, *Isaac Newton: A Biography* (New York: Scribner, 1934), 664.
[5]C. S. Lewis, "Christianity and Literature," *Genesis: Journal of the Society of Christians in the Arts, Inc.* 1, no. 2 (1975): 22.

The import of this reflection on our human calling to "till the garden" of this world with body, mind, and imagination is that the arts need no justification; they are good gifts of God, a basic part of the creation order. Our calling is simply to be thankful for these gifts of sub-creativity.

We may say, however, that there are five aspects of our God-given creativity, or five "callings" to direct us as we engage in the work of creating before the face of God, the great Creator who made us like himself and for himself:

- We are to seek to *glorify God* in all we do.
- We are designed to *find fulfillment for ourselves* in using, developing, and expressing the gifts God has so richly given us.
- We are to seek to *be of benefit to others*, so that they may be able to look at what we create and say of it, "It is good." The Christian artist always lives in community and is called to serve others in the development and expression of the gifts God has given to each one for the blessing of all.
- In being creative, we fulfill our human design by *exercising dominion* over the earth.
- We are called, in all we do, including in our creative work, to *set back the boundaries of the fall*, to restrain the abnormality of our present human life in its brokenness and sorrow and of our present world that is under the curse and therefore resists our dominion.

2

Imitation, the Heart of the Christian's Approach to Creativity

In becoming a Christian, a person bows before God as Creator, Lord, Judge, Redeemer, Lawgiver, and Teacher. In everything we recognize that we are to live from henceforth before the face of God. How will this recognition impact the way we think about the work of the arts? In acknowledging that we live in God's world and that we are his creatures, the Christian ought to have a rather more humble approach to the work of art than is sometimes found in the reflections of those artists who see themselves at the center of reality.

Shakespeare had this humility about his work, though if we consider both the dramas and the poetry that poured out from him, we might justly call him one of the greatest of human creators. The poet Dryden said of Shakespeare, "After God, he has created most." In polls done around the year 2000, Shakespeare was considered far and away the most significant human being of the previous millennium. Yet Shakespeare said of himself that he simply held "a mirror up to nature," and in all his writings there is no trace of arrogance or demand to be considered someone more special than others because of his creative gifts.

George Herbert, like Shakespeare a Christian, wrote in "The Forerunners,"

> True beauty dwells on high; ours is a flame
> But borrowed thence to light us thither.

Lewis comments on this understanding of the artist as being an imitator rather than an original creator, and in the process he challenges much contemporary reflection about the work of the artist:

> What are the key-words of modern criticism? *Creative*, with its opposite *derivative; spontaneity*, with its opposite *convention; freedom*, contrasted with *rules*. Great authors are innovators, pioneers, explorers; bad authors bunch in schools and follow models. Or again, great authors are always "breaking fetters" and "bursting bonds." They have personality, they "are themselves." I do not know whether we often think out the implication of such language into a consistent philosophy; but we certainly have a general picture of bad work flowing from conformity and discipleship, and of good work bursting out from certain centres of explosive force—apparently self-originating force—which we call men of genius.[1]

Lewis then draws our attention to the way in which the New Testament speaks about the Christian life in very different terms:

> Thus in Gal. iv. 19 Christ is to be "formed" inside each believer— the verb here used meaning to shape, to figure, or even to draw a sketch. In First Thessalonians (i. 6) Christians are told to imitate St. Paul and the Lord, and elsewhere (1 Cor. x. 33) to imitate St. Paul as he in his turn imitates Christ—thus giving us another stage of progressive imitation. Changing the metaphor we find that believers are to acquire the fragrance of Christ, *redolere Christum* (2 Cor. ii. 16); that the glory of God has appeared in the face of Christ as, at the creation, light appeared in the universe (2 Cor. iv. 6); and, finally, if my reading of a much disputed passage is correct, that a Christian is to Christ as a mirror to an object (2 Cor. iii. 18).

Lewis points out that thinking of oneself as "original" and as a "creator" is very close to summing up the reality of the fall, where humans turned from what is better and greater than

---

[1]This and the next several quotes are taken from C. S. Lewis, "Christianity and Literature," *Genesis: Journal of the Society of Christians in the Arts, Inc.* 1, no. 2 (1975): 18–20.

themselves—God, who is the Originator—to what is lesser and derived—themselves. Lewis then applies this biblical insight to the work of the writer and the artist:

> Applying this principle to literature, in its greatest generality, we should get as the basis of all critical theory the maxim that an author should never conceive of himself as bringing into existence beauty or wisdom that did not exist before, but simply and solely as trying to embody in terms of his own art some reflection of eternal Beauty and Wisdom.

Lewis comments on the difference between the Christian and the man who sees himself at the center of reality: "St. Augustine and Rousseau both write *Confessions*; but to the one his own temperament is a kind of absolute (*au moins je suis autre*), to the other it is 'a narrow house, too narrow for thee to enter—oh make it wide. It is in ruins—oh rebuild it.'"

Lewis explicitly acknowledges the similarities between a Christian view and a Platonic view of the arts as imitative of something transcendent. For the Platonist and neo-Platonist, this world is a copy, a shadow of the divine world above. The arts will not be satisfied with exploring what is found here—the copies—but will seek to enter into heaven itself to imitate the true origin of all that we see here on earth. Quoting Plotinus, Lewis says: "'The arts do not simply imitate what they see but re-ascend to those principles from which Nature herself is derived.' Art and Nature thus become rival copies of the same supersensual original, and there is no reason why Art should not be the better of the two."[2]

I am not suggesting, of course, that Platonic and Christian views of the arts are precisely the same. The point is simply this: both the Platonist and the Christian acknowledge that this world is dependent on something greater. As a Christian I acknowledge that all things, including myself, are made by God and that all things, including myself, live in dependence on God and for God.

---

[2]Plotinus, *Ennead*, 5.8.320, quoted in C. S. Lewis, *English Literature in the Sixteenth Century, Excluding Drama*, Oxford History of English Literature 3 (London: Oxford University Press, 1954), 320.

As an artist I will be glad to receive from above the pattern for my work—just as those who built the tabernacle and the temple did their work in obedience to God's ordering and in submission to the heavenly original that they copied.

Using Sir Philip Sidney as an example, Lewis further notes:

> The poet, unlike the historian, is not "captived to the truth of a foolish world," but can "deliver a golden." Sidney . . . inherited, in a Christianized form, the Platonic dualism. Nature was not the whole. Above earth was heaven; behind the phenomenal, the metaphysical. To that higher region the human soul belonged. The natural world, as Bacon said, was "in proportion inferior to the soul." The man who . . . improved on Nature, and painted what might be or ought to be, did not feel that he was retreating from reality into a merely subjective refuge; he was reascending from a world which he had a right to call "foolish" and asserting his divine origin.[3]

We may describe a Christian understanding of the arts in the following way: Our work in any field of the arts will be imitative. We will be thinking God's thoughts after him—painting with his colors; speaking with his gift of language; exploring and expressing his sounds and harmonies; working with his creation in all its glory, diversity, and in-built inventiveness. In addition, we will find ourselves longing to make known the beauty of life as it once was in Paradise, the tragedy of its present marring, and the hope of our final redemption. All great art will echo these three elements of Eden: (1) Eden in its original glory, (2) Eden that is lost to us, and (3) the promise that Eden will be restored. We will look later in some depth at this call of the artist to make "echoes of Eden."

I do not mean to suggest that there is no room for creativity or originality in a Christian understanding of the arts. Lewis thought it appropriate to use the term *sub-creation* for J. R. R. Tolkien's work *The Lord of the Rings*, for Tolkien devoted a lifetime to creating the world of Middle-earth in extraordinary depth and detail. Yet, he

---

[3]Lewis, *English Literature in the Sixteenth Century*, 320–21.

was, of course, dependent on this "first" creation, God's creation, as the original from which Tolkien "copied" all his remarkable ideas. So then, we may use the terms *creative* and *original* as long as we understand that we do not mean them in an absolute sense, for in everything we do, we act as those who are created and who are working within the boundaries of this created universe.

We can therefore take delight in this secondary sense of "sub-creation" as found in the work of a Christian poet who designs new forms (as did John Donne or T. S. Eliot); or the plays of a Christian dramatist whose work far supersedes that of his predecessors (as did Shakespeare's); or the compositions of a Christian musician who writes music in original styles (as did Bach); or the canvases of the Christian painter who breaks with tradition (as did Rembrandt or van Gogh). However, a Christian will just as gladly use forms already in existence if those forms fit the purposes and passions of any given work.

Another way to express this recognition of the secondary nature of all our art would be to understand that all creative work is a form of praise and worship: by creating we declare the glory of God, who made us in his likeness.

The Arts as More Than an Expression of the Self

These reflections on imitation rather than absolute originality for the artist lead us to a related issue. Since the Romantic period, beginning in the years after 1800, the arts have become increasingly a matter of mere self-expression. This arises from the sense of the artist as the one who sees to the very core of reality. In this view the artist becomes like God, just as Adam and Eve were tempted by the serpent to imagine that they could become rivals to God. The artist is seen as having a special sensibility that gives him or her a higher understanding of and deeper insight into the human condition, which therefore elevates the artist above the average person as one to be admired.

But the Christian who works in the arts will not presume to be the great revealer, another god, the prophet or priest of the age, a special mentor breaking new barriers. To do so would be to become the priest in a smaller and smaller cult. The more inward and purely self-expressive art becomes, the more inaccessible it is to others. For artistic communication to occur, art cannot be simply an expression of the self. True art must have some contact with life, with reality, with other people who exist alongside the artist. Lewis puts it something like this: "Great writing (and all great art) exists because there is a world not created by the writer."

In contrast to the Romantic view, artists need to see themselves as dependent on abilities they are born with, as dependent on others, and as dependent on the objective world around them. Christian artists need to regard themselves as creatures of God, using gifts given by God, delighting in the world made by God, needing the help of other artists, doing their work to the glory of God, and devoting their labors to the enrichment of the lives of others.

The Creativity of Others Helps Us Enter into God's Creativity

We are finite, and that is good, for this is the way God made us; yet God's world surrounds us with all its extraordinary variety, beauty, order, and richness. Lewis reflects on how we may experience more of the wonder of God's world as we read and so enter into someone else's perspective on this world. This is true in all the arts; each painter, sculptor, writer, composer, musician, or designer sees something of the world that we do not see, and so as we look or listen or read, we are enriched by each artist's vision. Lewis asks why we enjoy reading (and we may apply this to all the arts). He answers:

> The nearest I have yet got to an answer is that we seek an enlargement of our being. We want to be more than ourselves. Each of us by nature sees the whole world from one point of view with a perspective and a selectiveness peculiar to himself. And even when we build disinterested fantasies, they are saturated with, and limited by, our own psychology. To acquiesce in this particularity on the sensuous level—in other words, not to dis-

count perspective—would be lunacy. We should then believe that the railway line really grew narrower as it receded into the distance. But we want to escape the illusions of perspective on higher levels too. We want to see with other eyes, to imagine with other imaginations, to feel with other hearts, as well as with our own. We are not content to be Leibnitzian monads. We demand windows. Literature as Logos is a series of windows, even of doors. One of the things we feel after reading a great work is "I have got out." Or from another point of view, "I have got in"; pierced the shell of some other monad and discovered what it is like inside.[4]

Lewis points out how reading (or the enjoyment of any art-work) is similar to love, moral activity, and the exercise of the mind, for in each of these activities we are called out of ourselves into the life of another person. This would be a joy and an enlargement of us even if we were not fallen creatures, for we are told that even before the rebellion of our first ancestors, it was "not good for the man to be alone" (Gen. 2:18). God has so designed us that we need others to complement us in every aspect of our lives.

God has not made us to be isolated individuals who find fulfillment simply by ourselves, or even—and I say this carefully—only in relationship with him. He has made us for others so that, though finite persons, we together can reflect the unity and diversity within the godhead, and can take delight in the gifts, wisdom, and insight of our fellow men and women. The greatest commandment calls us to love God with heart and soul and mind and strength, and to love our neighbor as ourselves. God's Word teaches us that we know we love God by the reality of our love for other human persons.[5]

When we add to this the fact that we are fallen and that the essence of the fall is to worship and serve oneself, we begin to see how important are the arts, for they give us a wider and fuller view of God's good world. The arts enable us to look beyond ourselves and beyond the horizons of our own experience. They help us to stop being so self-centered. Lewis writes:

---

[4]C. S. Lewis, *An Experiment in Criticism* (Cambridge: Cambridge University Press, 1965), 137–38.
[5]See 1 John 4:7–12.

Good reading, therefore, though it is not essentially an affectional or moral or intellectual activity, has something in common with all three. In love we escape from our self into one other. In the moral sphere, every act of justice or charity involves putting ourselves in the other person's place and thus transcending our own competitive particularity. In coming to understand anything we are rejecting the facts as they are for us in favour of the facts as they are. The primary impulse of each is to maintain and aggrandize himself. The secondary impulse is to go out of the self, to correct its provincialism and heal its loneliness. In love, in virtue, in the pursuit of knowledge, and in the reception of the arts, we are doing this. Obviously this process can be described either as an enlargement or as a temporary annihilation of the self. But that is an old paradox; "he that loseth his life shall save it." . . .

This, so far as I can see, is the specific value or good of literature considered as Logos; it admits us to experiences other than our own. They are not, any more than our personal experiences, all equally worth having. Some, as we say, "interest" us more than others. The causes of this interest are naturally extremely various and differ from one man to another; it may be the typical (and we say "How true!") or the abnormal (and we say "How strange!"); it may be the beautiful, the terrible, the awe-inspiring, the exhilarating, the pathetic, the comic, or the merely piquant. Literature gives the entrée to them all. . . .

Literary experience heals the wound, without undermining the privilege, of individuality. There are mass emotions which heal the wound; but they destroy the privilege. In them our separate selves are pooled and we sink back into sub-individuality. But in reading great literature I become a thousand men and yet remain myself. Like the night sky in the Greek poem, I see with a myriad eyes, but it is still I who see. Here, as in worship, in love, in moral action, and in knowing, I transcend myself; and am never more myself than when I do.[6]

"Literature makes us feel more about things, and feel about more things." A friend attributed these words to Thomas De Quincey, the English essayist. I have not been able to confirm this attribu-

---

[6]Lewis, *An Experiment in Criticism*, 138–41.

tion, but anyone who loves to read will agree gladly that literature deepens and broadens our experience. What is true of literature is true of all the arts. In the enjoyment of others' creativity, I enter into a vision and richness beyond my own: "familiar things made new, new things made familiar," to paraphrase Samuel Johnson. Chesterton understood this and sums it up for us: "Fiction means the common things as seen by the uncommon people."[7] T. S. Eliot also writes of this as he thinks about the nature of poetry. The poet, he suggests, leads us into a new level of consciousness,

> making people more aware of what they feel already, and there-fore teaching them something about themselves. But he is not merely a more conscious individual than the others; he is also individually different from other people, and from other poets too, and can make his readers share consciously in new feelings which they had not experienced before.[8]

In this expansion of the self, the arts are indeed like love or moral action. One gives oneself to another, yet is never more fully oneself.

Art by Christians and by Non-Christians

An important question arises here that takes us back to an idea brought up at the beginning of this book: Should Christians only enjoy the art of fellow Christians? The question might imply that Christians make better artists than non-Christians, which seems absurd! But many believers speak as if it is impossible for the Christian to enjoy or be edified by the creative works of unbeliev-ers. As I pointed out earlier, the truth is that there is not a single Christian in the world who does not daily benefit from the creative gifts and hard work of the unbelievers around him or her. Our clothes, our food, our homes, our public buildings, our transport, our furnishings, our machinery, our technology—the greater part of all of this has been designed and made by people who are not Christians. Besides enjoying the practical *utility* of many of these

---

[7]G. K. Chesterton, *Charles Dickens: A Critical Study* (New York: Dodd Mead, 1906), 84.
[8]T. S. Eliot, "On Poetry and Poets," quoted in *Reading Literature: Some Christian Approaches*, ed. David Barratt and Roger Pooley (Leicester, UK: UCCF Literary Studies Group, 1985), 8.

things, there is no single believer anywhere in the world who does not also enjoy daily the *beauty* of design apparent in many of these essential parts of our lives.

On even the briefest reflection of the daily benefit Christians receive from the work of non-Christians, it is obvious that God has given his creative gifts to believers and unbelievers alike. Scripture acknowledges this in many ways, and we should need no other evidence than the insistence of God's Word that all human persons are made in his image (see Psalm 8 once more, or James 3:9–10).

In Acts 14:17, we see Paul talking to the idolatrous pagans in the city of Lystra about God's generosity. He says, "[God] has not left himself without a testimony: He has shown kindness by giving you rain from heaven and crops in their seasons" (NIV). Jesus calls us to be like our heavenly Father, who gives his good gifts to the believer and the unbeliever, the righteous and the wicked (Matt. 5:43–48). The writer of Proverbs declares that God's wisdom raises her voice not just to the people of Israel but to the whole human race so that there might be good laws and just rule in every nation (Prov. 8:1–4, 15–16). In 1 Kings 5, we read how God is pleased that Solomon is hiring the finest craftsmen of the day, unbelievers sent by Hiram, king of Tyre, to build the temple and to work on its interior design.

This is a particularly interesting example, for it teaches us that it is perfectly appropriate for us to use the gifts of non-Christians to help us build our houses of worship or to aid our worship in other ways (we will return to this issue later). On this subject of what is generally called the "common grace" of God, John Calvin writes with great passion about the folly and blasphemy of denying that God has given his gifts liberally to unbelievers:

> Therefore, in reading profane authors, the admirable light of truth displayed in them should remind us, that the human mind, however much fallen and perverted from its original integrity, is still adorned and invested with admirable gifts from its Creator. If we reflect that the Spirit of God is the only fountain of truth, we will be careful, as we would avoid offering insult to him, not

to reject or condemn truth wherever it appears. In despising the gifts, we insult the Giver.[9]

And again:

> The sum of the whole is this: From a general survey of the human race, it appears that one of the essential properties of our nature is reason, which distinguishes us from the lower animals, just as these by means of sense are distinguished from inanimate objects. For although some individuals are born without reason, that defect does not impair the general kindness of God [the Battles translation here has "general grace"; the French is *la grace generale de Dieu*], but rather serves to remind us, that whatever we retain ought justly to be ascribed to the divine indulgence. Had God not so spared us, our revolt would have carried along with it the entire destruction of nature. In that some excel in acuteness, and some in judgment, while others have greater readiness in learning some peculiar art, God, by this variety commends his favor toward us, lest any one should presume to arrogate to himself that which flows from his mere liberality. For whence is it that one is more excellent than another, but that in a common nature the grace of God is specially displayed [Battles translates this as "why is one person more excellent than another? Is it not to display in common nature God's special grace?" The French is *la grace special de Dieu.*] in passing by many and thus proclaiming that it is under obligation to none. We may add, that each individual is brought under particular influences according to his calling.[10]

Calvin in this passage speaks of "general grace" and a form of "special grace" as he reflects on the generous giving of gifts by God to the whole human race. He is quite happy to acknowledge that in many areas of human activity unbelievers may be more gifted and have more wisdom than believers. If you are troubled by this statement, just think of the planes in which you fly, the buildings that you admire or in which you live and work, the technology or

---

[9]John Calvin, *Institutes of the Christian Religion*, trans. Henry Beveridge, rev. ed. (Peabody, MA: Hendrickson, 2008), 2.2.15.
[10]Ibid., 2.2.17.

medical care from which you benefit. Almost certainly the majority of these have been designed and made by non-Christians. This truth should not trouble us at all, but rather cause us to magnify the grace of God, who gives to all so generously. The question we need to ask about any human artifact is not, Is this made by a Christian or a non-Christian? but rather the question that Genesis 1 prompts us to ask: Is this good?

Arts and Crafts

Another question is the relationship between what tend to be called "arts" (such as music, literature, and painting) and "crafts" (such as the making of household furnishings, clothes, and buildings). Hans Rookmaaker, for many years professor of art history at the Free University of Amsterdam and a director of the L'Abri Fellowship in Holland, wrote very helpfully on this subject. Rookmaaker pointed out that at one time—through the Middle Ages and beyond the Reformation—what we now call the arts were all considered crafts; artists were workmen and working women like any other laborers. Young people were apprenticed in painting or music just as they were in furniture making or metalwork or dyeing. Art was simply the beauty that one expected to find in things made by skilled craftsmen and artisans.

Christians were a part of this cultural outlook, recognizing their abilities in these areas as gifts and callings from God. The result was a great wealth of music, literature, painting, sculpture, architecture, furniture, and many other things that people still flock to see, hear, and enjoy. Consider the examples of Bach, Rembrandt, and Shakespeare—each an outstanding artisan in his particular craft.

Perceptions about the arts began to change during the Romantic period. Art came to be seen as "fine art" or "high culture"; the crafts came to be considered inferior. The arts were disconnected from life, and the artist was deemed a kind of noble genius. What were some of the results of this shift in thinking about the nature of the arts? Here we will summarize some of the points that Rookmaaker makes in his writing on this subject (see, in particular, his essay *Art Needs No Justification*).[11]

One result of this shift was that art became museum art instead of artistically made objects that were part of the everyday life. We now go to museums to see the works of "great artists," works that may be beautiful and meaningful in many ways, but have been set apart from the ordinary by their status as art. Contrast that with the great outpouring of paintings that decorated the churches and public buildings in the late medieval period or at the time of the Renaissance. These works were part of people's lives; wherever they went in the course of a day or a week, they met with artistic works created to beautify everyday existence. With the redefinition of art, however, this became less and less the case.

Along with this shift in thinking and the divorce of artistic endeavors from the everyday, art also became very expensive. Unlike the contemporaries of Michelangelo or Leonardo da Vinci, the common man and woman had very little access to the works of the great artists until the rise of public museums.

In addition, there developed a separation of fine art from commercial art or entertainment art, though in every field, a few artists managed to transcend these divisions. Toulouse-Lautrec, Johann Strauss, Duke Ellington—these are some who bridged that gap between art per se and commercial or entertainment art. Largely because of technology, nowadays we are able to enjoy at a popular level some of the works of the great artists of a previous time— artisans who did not think of themselves as working away at some "higher calling," but who saw themselves as serving the men and women of their day with the gifts God had given them. Think here of the excellent recent films based on the plays of William Shakespeare or the novels of Jane Austen, which are fine examples of how great art and commercial art can come together, as were the original works of these two authors.

---

[11] Hans Rookmaaker, *Art Needs No Justification* (Downers Grove, IL: InterVarsity, 1978).

Another consequence of this separation of arts and crafts is the alienation of most ordinary people from the arts (in contrast to the audiences of Shakespeare's plays, which were enjoyed by queen—and later king—and commoner alike). Along with this alienation of ordinary people there has arisen a special class of "art interpreters"—reviewers and critics whose job it is to educate the rest of us so that we are able to understand the arts. Often there is a vast gulf between what the art interpreters claim is good art and what ordinary people enjoy.

When the BBC did a poll on the greatest author of the twentieth century, the public overwhelmingly chose J. R. R. Tolkien and his work *The Lord of the Rings*. Many critics were outraged, as they had expected James Joyce or Virginia Woolf to be chosen. They demanded that the poll be done again and the questions changed to favor their notions of great literature. No matter how the questions were asked, Tolkien still won!

Another example is the BBC poll on which book most influenced British women. Instead of a work by Virginia Woolf, Germaine Greer, or some other heroine of many feminist reviewers, the outright winner was Jane Austen's *Pride and Prejudice*. More recently, when Lee Child was awarded finest "Crime Fiction Writer" of 2011 for his outstanding Jack Reacher novels, the great detective-fiction writer P. D. James praised Child publicly for the quality of his work, then added wryly that she feared Child would never win the Booker Prize for finest novel of the year.[12] One of the judges on the Booker panel had remarked that a crime-fiction writer would win the Booker Prize over his dead body.

Romantic notions of art create practical difficulties for artists and art students who are sensible enough to see the problems of this approach. Indeed, we currently see a crisis in the arts that leads to the question, Why am I working at this? By the Romantic vision of art, the artist is driven inward to find his or her identity in and through the work produced. But a problem arises: what if one finds only emptiness inside?

---

[12]P. D. James has written an outstanding series of novels with the detective Adam Dalgliesh as one of her major characters. Many of these books have been turned into excellent television series.

The Romantic conception of artists as tortured geniuses expressing their innermost being creates particular difficulty for Christians who see the arts as the epitome and clearest expression of the non-Christian spirit of the age. This generates a reaction among the vast majority of Christians and raises two problems that constantly confront the believer who senses God's calling to be an artist.

First, art is considered by many in our churches to be unnecessary and unspiritual, even worldly. Therefore, Christians who desire to be artists are told, "Leave art to the pagans. Our Christian calling is to be spiritual and to bear witness to Christ." But even if we take this negative attitude toward the arts, we still find that art is inescapably part of our lives. Anyone who thinks about the presentation of food on a plate or what colors of flowers to grow in their garden is acknowledging that human beings cannot escape the arts.

Second, the Christian who perseveres and enters the arts has to face all sorts of criticisms: the charge of hedonism, of worldliness, of being sinful or carnal. Artists are often considered lazy, for art is not "real work." The artist is thought to be in danger from the world. A young believer who persists in such a calling may be told, "If you have to be an artist, then at least use your art for evangelistic purposes. This can be your only justification for pursuing such a life."

How are we as Christians to respond to such charges, criticisms, and challenges? We do need to make a response for the sake of Christians who have been gifted by God and who wish to pursue this calling. And our response should including the following:

- *Art needs no justification.* It is simply a gift of God, part of his created reality, to be received like any other gift—with gratitude.
- *We must not say that "art is for art's sake," for this is the Romantic heresy.* Art is to be tied to the reality of God's creation and to our human calling to live as his image bearers.
- *The Christian artist will regard himself or herself as a craftsperson.* Artists will see themselves not as self-serving visionaries, but as ordinary humans (that is glorious enough!) with a particular

calling from God to serve him and their fellow humans by working with words, music, color, stone, metal, and so on.

- *Most importantly, the Christian in the arts will be committed to humility.* The true artist does *not* say, "I will be an artist, an inspired voice of the gods" (this is too religious a claim), or the "revealer of truth," as if a prophet, or a "self-revealing genius" (these suggest that only the artist can truly see reality). Rather, the true artist sees his or her work within the context of and as a subset of God's larger and infinitely more creative work. The true artist values something more than self. The true artist holds up a mirror to what God has made.

3

Building a Christian Understanding of the Artist's Calling

Now that we have explored various attitudes toward the arts and seen how human artistic endeavors are actually echoes of the greater creative activity of God, we are prepared to ask several questions that will help us develop a truly Christian understanding of the calling of the artist.

Are There "Christian Subjects," and Is There "Christian Art"?

The expressions "Christian subjects" and "Christian art" are often used, and we need to ask ourselves what such language means. Do we mean that there are particular subjects, and only those subjects, that are appropriate for a Christian artist to explore in painting, music, writing, or any other area of the arts? Do we believe that only some particular kinds of work should be called "Christian art"?

I suppose we might mean that "Christian art" is art designed for use in worship or devotion, such as hymns, sacred music, devotional literature, meditations, prayers, paintings and banners for churches, stained glass windows, and the like. There is, of course, a need for such art, but rather than lumping it into a separate category called "Christian," we must learn that this kind of art will have to be judged by the same criteria as all other art. C. S. Lewis is once again a great help to us:

> The rules for writing a good passion play or a good devotional lyric are simply the rules for writing tragedy or lyric in general:

success in sacred literature depends on the same qualities of structure, suspense, variety, diction, and the like which secure success in secular literature. And if we enlarge the idea of Christian Literature to include not only literature on sacred themes but all that is written by Christians for Christians to read, then, I think, Christian Literature can exist only in the same sense in which Christian cookery might exist. It would be possible, and it might be edifying, to write a Christian cookery book. Such a book would exclude dishes whose preparation involves unnecessary human labour or animal suffering, and dishes excessively luxurious. That is to say, its choice of dishes would be Christian. But there could be nothing specifically Christian about the actual cooking of the dishes included. Boiling an egg is the same process whether you are a Christian or a Pagan. In the same way, literature written by Christians for Christians would have to avoid mendacity, cruelty, blasphemy, pornography, and the like, and it would aim at edification in so far as edification was proper to the kind of work in hand. But whatever it chose to do would have to be done by the means common to all literature; it could succeed or fail only by the same excellences and the same faults as all literature; and its literary success or failure would never be the same thing as its obedience or disobedience to Christian principles.[1]

A second possible use of such terms as "Christian art" is to describe art that has what we might call "Christian content." By this is usually meant art containing depictions of biblical scenes or scenes from church history. However, people generally have a narrow view of this type of art and usually mean sacred, holy, edifying, or even "nice" works of art ("nice," for most people, meaning "what I like"). Yet, compare this to some scenes in the Bible that are not obviously edifying on first reading. Think of the rape of Tamar (2 Samuel 13), for instance; or the gang rape and death of the Levite's concubine, whose body is cut up, and the subsequent war (Judges 19); or the Song of Songs, with its explicit sex and graphic nudity; or the book of Ecclesiastes, with its pessimistic themes. In

---

[1]C. S. Lewis, "Christianity and Literature," *Genesis: Journal of the Society of Christians in the Arts, Inc.* 1, no. 2 (1975): 14.

other words, there are sections of the Bible that would seem to fail this test for "Christian art" or "Christian subjects."

A third way to use this language is to refer to art that is didactic, teaching us spiritual or evangelistic lessons. But, again, many scenes in the Bible itself would fail this test (see again the passages mentioned above). There are no "spiritual" lessons in the Song of Songs, though many Christians, uncomfortable with the idea that God might have included in his infallible Word a book that appears to be mainly about sex, have tried to make it a book about the marriage of the soul to Christ or the union of the church to her Lord. Of course, some art will be "spiritual" in this sense, but some will not. Art does not need this justification for it to be considered good art—art that a Christian can produce or enjoy.

A fourth way this language is used is to refer to art produced by Christians. But this is also problematic. Some of the best-loved hymn tunes, for example, were borrowed from folk melodies rather than composed specially for the purpose of worship; think of the tunes we use for "Fairest Lord Jesus," "Amazing Grace," "What Wondrous Love Is This?" and "I Cannot Tell." In addition, some of the greatest composers of sacred music were not believers (Vaughan Williams is an example), and many great hymn tunes were taken from the music of composers who were not believers, or from contexts that were not "Christian" (such as Beethoven's rousing "Ode to Joy" or Sibelius's beautiful "Finlandia," both of which are used for dearly loved hymns).

This principle of accepting art by unbelievers is also borne out within the Bible itself. The book of Proverbs contains many sayings from ancient Egypt and from other nations outside of Israel, sayings included in the scriptural text not because they are all by believers or by Hebrews, but simply because they are true wisdom. Proverbs 8 affirms this very point by declaring that God's wisdom raises her voice to the whole human race. Another example is the poetic form of the Psalms. In the Psalms and in other biblical poetry in both the Old and New Testaments (see Mary's song, for example), we find that one of the primary poetic forms is the use of parallelism of content. This is very different from the use of rhyme and regular rhythm, what we might call a parallelism of structure (rather than content, which is the poetic form we often use in English and most other Western literature). The form we find in biblical poetry is not unique to Israel, for the structure of the Psalms is not dropped from heaven, but is rather a culturally common form in Israel's part of the ancient world.

In addition, many of the metaphors used—even for God—are part of the poetic language of the surrounding culture and are not unique to the Old Testament. We find some of those metaphors used of Baal, designated the "storm God" by the Canaanites, one common one describing God as he who makes the clouds his chariot and who rides on the wings of the wind. This should not bother us any more than it would if we discovered that the most beautiful and acoustically perfect church building in our city was designed by a non-Christian architect, or if we discovered that this non-Christian architect had donated his services to the members of the church.

At the most basic level, when it comes to the arts, we must hold Christians to the same standards of judgment as we would any other artist—just as we hold Christians in medicine, or teaching, or business, or any other calling to an objective set of standards. I would not want to take my child, ill with leukemia, to a doctor just because he claimed to be a Christian. I would try to find out whether he was a well-trained and competent physician. The same should be true if I am looking for an architect, an interior designer, music to play or listen to, a novel to read, a play to see, a movie to watch, or an artist or artistic work in any field of the arts. I will be looking first for quality rather than for the claim of faith.

This means, then, that we might do well to speak of Christian artists, or of Christians who are called to be artists, in the same way that we speak of Christians who are doctors, lawyers, teachers, homemakers, or cooks, rather than speaking of Christian medicine, Christian cooking, and so on. Then, once we learn to speak this way, our challenge to all believers will be to pursue their callings with heart, soul, mind, and strength to the glory of God so that the dedication of their lives and the quality of their work brings honor to their Maker.

What Will This Mean for Topics?

The above conclusion will also help us as we think about appropriate topics for the Christian who is an artist. We may put it bluntly: there are no secular topics. All creation is God's and therefore is proper material for artistic expression. But, you may respond, "There is much that is bad about this world and that therefore does not reveal the perfectly holy character of God." This is of course true, and so we may add that the world and human life in all its fallenness and brokenness is appropriate subject matter for the Christian artist, just as it is appropriate subject matter for the Word of God. We may add further that the hope for redemption from this state of brokenness is also fit material for the artist.

In fact, we may propose as a principle that the themes of all great art—whether produced by Christians or non-Christians—are the world and human life as they came from the hand of God; the world and human life as they now are subject to sorrow, sin, and death; and the world and human life as we long for and look forward to their restoration. Which theme predominates will vary from piece to piece in the work of any particular artist, and will vary from artist to artist depending on his or her belief system and experience of life. I refer to this reality as "echoes of Eden": echoes of creation, fall, and redemption in the arts.

It is hard to imagine Tamar in her desolation after her rape, for instance, writing upbeat songs of joy. Indeed, it would be false if she were to write and sing such songs—unless they were about her ultimate redemption and the wiping away of her tears. Her life in this world was ruined by the wicked act of her half brother, and so, even any songs of joy she might have written and sung would have been full of tears as long as she walked in this broken world.

The character Aragorn in *The Lord of the Rings* makes a profound statement. He says that there are sorrows in this world so great that their tears are never wiped away in this life. Any of us who has lost a child to accident, crime, or sickness, or who has a family member or friend for whom this is the case, will know the truth of Aragorn's words.

This means, too, that there will be no room for sentimentality in a Christian approach to the arts. Hagiographies, for example, which many Christian biographies are, have no place here. The Bible itself does not glorify human beings in this way, nor does it pretend that their lives were perfect. Rather, it speaks with deep and sometimes brutal honesty about the failures of the people of God. Think of how David is described as "a man after [God's] heart" (Acts 13:22), yet we read his story and see how deeply flawed he was. Would any responsible father want his sons to live with such sexual laxness as David showed? Would any good father be pleased if he raised his sons as poorly as David raised his, so that he would not even rebuke his eldest son and heir for an abominable rape of his own half sister?

I do not mean to suggest that God's gracious love for David was misplaced. God forbid! Without the mercy and forgiveness of God, David and you and I would all be lost. I simply make the point that David is a man with clay feet—like us all. This, of course, is why we find reading the Bible to be such a comfort, for God's Word is about people like us, not about plaster saints.

Related to this need for Christian biographies to be truthful, as well as kind, is the need for realism in the presentation of Christ as truly human. We have all seen paintings of Christ in which his humanity is diminished to make him appear "sweet."

A favorite book of mine is *Michael O'Halloran* by Gene Stratton-Porter. In the story, the house of a wealthy woman has been turned into a children's hospital. Her estranged husband visits his former home for the first time since its transformation, and his wife's.

> At the top of the steps leading to the entrance stood a marble group of heroic proportions. . . . It was a seated figure of Christ, but cut with the face of a man of his station [a working man], occupation [carpenter / fisherman], and race [Jewish], garbed in a simple robe, and in his arms, at his knees, leaning against him, a group of children: the lean, sick and ailing, such as were carried to him for healing. Cut in the wall above it in large gold-filled letters was the admonition: "Suffer little children to come unto me."

That group was the work of a student and a thinker who could carry an idea to a logical conclusion, and then carve it from marble. The thought it gave James Minturn, arrested before it, was not the stereotyped idea of Christ, not the conventional reproduction of childhood. It impressed on Mr. Minturn's brain that the man of Galilee has lived in the form of other men of his day, and that such a face, filled with infinite compassion, was much stronger and more forceful than that of the mild feminine countenance he had been accustomed to associating with the Savior.[2]

Jesus was indeed morally perfect and was God in the flesh; but the Scripture also teaches us that he was fully human and that he lived a normal life with his family in his particular cultural setting. In addition, he had a mortal body with all the accompanying flaws and weaknesses of our mortality. Faithfulness to Scripture requires the Christian artist to represent Jesus as he was, not in some idealized form.

This principle of representing things as they are is a matter of obedience and honesty. Simple integrity constrains us to communicate faithfully and truthfully not only about the Lord himself and other people whose stories appear in the Bible, but also about our current human condition. Honest art will delineate human shame as well as human glory, not because we wish to wallow in that shame, but because it represents the truth about who we always are as long as this life endures.

Of course, the Christian artist should also be ready, when it is appropriate, to communicate faith boldly and clearly, or to say simply and plainly, "My God and King!"[3] We have many glorious examples of this in the poetry of George Herbert, John Donne, Gerard Manley Hopkins, and T. S. Eliot.

Is Representational Art Forbidden by the Second Commandment?

The open declaration of Christian truth and the honoring of God's name lead to another question. How can we depict or represent

---

[2]Gene Stratton-Porter, *Michael O'Halloran* (Garden City, NY: Doubleday, Page, 1915), 355.
[3]A phrase from the first line of George Herbert's poem "The Elixir."

God? Is representation forbidden in the visual arts or in drama on stage or in the movies, or even in fiction? Some of us have seen William Blake's paintings, such as "The Ancient of Days." Many more will have seen either the originals or reproductions of some of Rembrandt's pictures of Christ as he taught and interacted with people, as he was raised on the cross, or as he met with the disciples after the resurrection. Most of us will have read, and now watched, Lewis's representation of Christ as the lion Aslan in the Narnia stories. Were these painters, writers, and filmmakers dishonoring God and disobeying his Word?

We all are familiar with the commandment that we are not to make a graven image or representation of God (or of anything in heaven above or on the earth beneath). This seems straightforward—and if this were all that the second commandment stated, we would have to conclude that all representational art (not only of God, but of anything else in creation) is forbidden by this law. This, incidentally, is the view of the most radical forms of Islam (for example, the Taliban or the Wahabi movement). However, if we read the whole of God's commandment about graven images, we see that what it forbids is the making of a representation and then bowing down to it and worshipping it. In other words, it is idolatry, not representation in and of itself, that is prohibited.

This is simple to demonstrate by reflecting on the context in which the commandment was given to Moses. The same Lord who gave the second commandment against representation for the purpose of worship also commissioned many works of art specifically for his houses of worship. There were to be representations of cherubim (things in heaven above) in both the tabernacle and the temple; representations of pomegranates, almond blossoms, bells (things created by God and by man on the earth beneath) in the tabernacle; and lions, bulls, lilies, gourds, palm trees, wreaths, wheels, and other things in the temple. All these were designed at God's command, some according to exact instructions given by him, others with considerable artistic freedom.

Some Christians attempt to resolve this issue of representational art by insisting that we no longer need such art now; they see it as "carnal," "unspiritual," or given specifically "for a time of spiritual immaturity or infancy." This view, however, is itself unbiblical, for the Word of God tells us that both the tabernacle and the temple were patterned after a heavenly design, and the basic requisition was given by God himself.

Nor will it do to declare that we only need the spoken and written Word now that Christ is come. This is the view of some believers who regard the Old Testament period as a time of spiritual infancy, and who consider that all visible, physical, and imaginative elements of worship are now completely unnecessary. Now, they argue, is the age of the Spirit; then, the people of Israel saw through a glass darkly; now, in comparison, we see face-to-face, for in Christ the formerly invisible things of God have been clearly made known. This presentation of our situation is partially accurate, for it stresses the wonder of the knowledge we now have because the Son of God became incarnate. But this approach also misses some profoundly important points.

Think of the book of Revelation. When the apostle John saw Christ in his glory, his imagination was fired to try to express what he saw so that we too may gain a glimpse of what he was privileged to witness. When we do ultimately see the Lord face-to-face, heaven itself will contain not only Christ but also the cherubim and all the other realities that the tabernacle and temple decorations represented. We will see him visibly and physically. We will see the cherubim. And, most probably, we will find other representations in heaven as well, even though we will be in the presence of the realities.

In fact, we might say that all the sacraments, representations, and symbols we have been given will find fulfillment in the kingdom to come; they will not disappear, but will be fully present in all their glory. We will partake of the marriage supper of the Lamb, and the Lord's Supper will then find its consummation, for Christ himself will serve us at his table. The tree of life will also be present for the healing of the nations. Christians who think that sacraments and symbols are unnecessary now for the truly spiritual believer need to recognize that the day will come when they will rejoice in these sacraments and symbols even while living in the full reality that the sacraments and symbols represent to us.

The key here, of course, is that we ourselves will still be physical beings in the new heavens and the new earth rather than disembodied spirits. Therefore, we may conclude that physical representations of heavenly and spiritual things are eternally appropriate, for God created us to be eternally bodied.

This leads to another important issue: what about representations of the Godhead in the visual arts and in literature? Are these necessarily blasphemous and idolatrous? What exactly is forbidden by the second commandment when it comes to representing or imagining God himself? Consider all the paintings people have made of Jesus, all the Christmas cards with manger scenes and the infant Christ, all the crèches, all the literary presentations of Christ (such as Aslan the lion). Are all of these idolatry? In many of our homes a crèche is set out for the celebration of Christmas. Is this idolatrous because it contains a small wooden figure of the infant Christ? Is this rough carving, and are all of these other mentioned representations of Christ, blasphemous? Again, the answer here is not quite as obvious as some suggest.

Think of the many images and metaphors used for God in Scripture. God is a shepherd, a physician, the owner of a vineyard, one who rides his chariot in the clouds. Christ is Vine, Door, Bridegroom, Lion, and Lamb. Genesis, using metaphorical language that suggests a bird, describes the Spirit brooding over the waters; and the Spirit also appears in the form of a dove. When we read such images, is it possible for us to reflect on them without imagining a form in our minds? I do not think so, for feeding the imagination is, without any doubt, the very purpose of this language.

Take the time to open Ezekiel 1 or Revelation 1 and ask yourself whether it is possible to read these chapters without picturing in your mind what Ezekiel and John are describing. In both cases, the writers struggle with words to represent something of what they have seen in their prophetic visions. If it were truly illegitimate to represent the Lord to us, then these descriptions would not be in Scripture. In fact, we may go further and suggest that because these word pictures are given to us in Scripture, it is appropriate for us to have paintings or sculptures that include representations of Jesus, and also to have acted representations of Jesus in plays and movies. What is inappropriate is to use any of these representations as an object of worship. That which signifies should never be confused with what it actually represents as if it were, in truth, the Lord himself and were to be treated as if it were the Lord. A representation of God is never to be worshipped as God himself.

Thinking about this issue at an even deeper level, we have to acknowledge that the incarnation itself does, of course, give the second person of the Godhead a particular physical form. The Son of God was incarnate in the likeness of man. And not a generic man, but an actual individual person, a specific man, just like any other man we meet every day—apart, of course, from Jesus's moral perfection and his full conformity to the likeness of God.

This means that Jesus, the God-man, could be seen, heard, and touched. People met him and went away with a visual image in their minds and hearts of who he was and what he looked like. This cannot have been a problem. Likewise, no one would suppose that Jesus's mother was disobeying the commandment against images when she cradled her infant son in her lap and, her eyes closed, thought about him with love; or that she later was sinning whenever she pictured Jesus in her mind. In the same way, who can doubt that the disciples and all those whom Jesus healed or taught kept glad memories of his face and form in their minds? We are told by Scripture that Mary pondered all the things that happened and treasured them in her heart. Luke informs us that he spoke to the eyewitnesses of the events and episodes in Jesus's life that he, Luke, describes. John writes with amazement of the privilege granted him, and others, that they were able to hear and see and touch the eternal Word of God because he took on flesh (1 John 1:1–3):

> That which was from the beginning, which we have heard, which we have seen with our eyes, which we have looked upon and have touched with our hands, concerning the word of life—the

life was made manifest, and we have seen it, and testify to it and proclaim to you the eternal life, which was with the Father and was made manifest to you—that which we have seen and heard we proclaim also to you.

Who can doubt or deny that John, when he wrote those words, had in mind specific memories of that beloved face and form? Seeing Jesus, the Son of God, very God of very God, and remembering him cannot have been for his contemporaries a violation of the second commandment, nor will it be for us when we shall see him face-to-face one day. Surely we cannot imagine that having seen him in his glory we will ever forget his appearance!

If Jesus had become incarnate in our own time, photographs could have been taken of him. We have to suppose that some of the children he played with as a young boy had artistic gifts and might have made sketches of him; or that later in his life a few of the many thousands who heard him speak might have made pictures of scenes of his teaching, just as our children's story Bibles have such pictures. In other words, we are saying that it must be acceptable to visualize Christ, simply because he became incarnate and was visible and, of course, still is visible and will forever be visible—for the incarnation was not a temporary appearance but an eternal embodying of the second person of the Trinity.

Consequently, we all have pictures of Jesus in our minds, first of all because he was fully human, and second, because of the vivid word pictures in Scripture. Indeed, much of the time when we think about Jesus and events in his life, we picture him, and we do this because it is completely natural for us to think this way. This means that all that is happening when we see a painting, sculpture, or acted portrayal of Jesus is that we get to see someone else's picture of Jesus. As long as it is faithful to Scripture, and as long as the intention of the artist is not to encourage worship of the image, surely this can only enrich our understanding of our Lord. The Narnia stories are a lovely example of this; we are given Lewis's rich insight into the glory of Christ to enlarge our own understanding. The paintings of Rembrandt are also helpful portraits to aid those of us who cannot express visually our sense of Jesus's humanity with the same extraordinary genius that God gave to Rembrandt.

What about representation in drama? Again, this subject cannot be dismissed as lightly as it often is. God himself uses dramatic signs to communicate to us. Consider the rainbow, or the whole sacrificial system, or the Passover. The Lord's Supper and baptism are simple dramas displaying for us the nature of our redemption through Christ. The Old Testament is full of stories that are enactments in history of what God himself has done and will one day do. See the story of Abraham sacrificing Isaac, the life of David, or the life of Joseph—each of these historical records pictures dramatically for us what God would do one day when Christ would come into the world. The incarnation itself is the greatest drama ever imagined or told, and whenever a preacher speaks about the incarnation, death, and resurrection of Jesus, he is rehearsing this drama for those who are listening.

We also have in Scripture several examples of the prophets using drama to aid their spoken words. See the examples of Isaiah (8:1–4; 20:1–6), Jeremiah (13:1–11; 16:1–9; 18:1–11; 19:1–13), and Ezekiel (4:1–17; 5:1–4). Given these biblical illustrations of God commanding the use of dramatic actions and signs to go with the spoken word, how can we possibly argue that the use of drama is always an unspiritual accompaniment to the proclaimed Word? While drama can be abused by becoming a mere show designed only for human appeal or entertainment, there is no biblical justification for frowning upon or condemning an *appropriate* use of drama within the context of the preaching of God's Word.

What about Abstract Art?

I want to touch just briefly on an issue that might seem at the opposite end of the spectrum from the issue of representation. If it is indeed right and good to represent things in heaven and on earth in our writing, drama, films, painting, and sculpture, including even the Lord himself, how should we think about abstract painting, sculpture, tapestry, and other visual forms of artistic expression? Some Christians think that all abstract art is somehow dishonoring to God and is necessarily uncreative. However, just reflect on some of the art in the tabernacle and temple; it is not all strictly representational. Consider as examples the seven-branched candelabra (almond branches and blossoms, but clearly not an exact likeness) or the pomegranates in various unrealistic colors on the garments of the high priest.

If we turn our eyes to God's creation, we are constantly met with sights that have the appearance of abstraction. Think of every sunrise or sunset you have ever seen—each one is different and changes every second, producing a constantly shifting series of abstract designs made by the greatest master of all abstract painters! Think of moving sand dunes, or waves on the sea, or branches against the sky, or fall colors. Everywhere we look, if we have eyes to see, we can begin to understand a little of where the abstract artist finds inspiration.

4

How Do We Judge the Arts?

In this chapter we turn to another area about which Christians express a variety of passionate and conflicting views. Often in magazine articles, on the radio and television, and in the pulpit, we find preachers and commentators condemning all sorts of literature, music, visual art, theater, and films. "No Christian should watch this movie . . . listen to this music . . . read this book." Certainly we should acknowledge that it is appropriate for us to test everything, to hold fast to that which is good, and to abstain from every form of evil, for Scripture commands us to do this. (In the context in 1 Thess. 5:20–22, these words of Paul are written about the discernment of prophecy, but we may quite appropriately apply them to the way we think about the arts as well.)

So, then, discernment is necessary. The question is, how are we to set about the task of testing everything and holding fast to that which is good? As was mentioned earlier there are objective qualities by which we all, every day, judge and then make choices about what food to purchase and eat, which doctor to see, which automobile to buy or lease. In the same way there are objective standards by which we can judge any work of art, whether in music, literature, filmmaking, painting, sculpture, dance, or any other field. Our knowledge of such standards is partly a matter of giftedness, intuition, experience, and common sense—just as with the examples of food, medical practitioners, or automobiles.

But the recognition of these standards is also, and perhaps even more so, a result of training and practice. We need to be taught about what food is nutritious and how to discern what is fresh and which additives are problematic for our health. We need help in making decisions about medical options or in purchasing a car (especially if, like me, one is completely ignorant of mechanical matters!). In this the arts are like any other field of human endeavor. Some matters are very simple for us all. Those who flock to Naples's beach each day to watch the sun go down over the Gulf and who marvel at it and often applaud as the magnificent globe retires from sight have not needed art lessons to appreciate the beauty and glory on display! Enjoying such a marvel comes with our humanity as God's image bearers and with the gift of sight. Yet we all know that our appreciation of the arts needs direction, encouragement, training, and practice. We will gain more from a concert or from watching a movie when we know a little about how the music or the film has been crafted and performed.

But the main point I wish to make here is that the arts are not above judgment, nor is the artist. If I do not like a book, why should I read it? The same with listening to music or with watching a movie—we all make judgments about what we want to see or hear or read. This is, of course, partly a matter of personal preference, but there is more to it than simply my likes and dislikes.

Criteria for Judging the Arts

So, how do we set about judging the arts and discerning what we want to see or hear or read? The following are the beginnings of a suggested list of appropriate criteria.

The Presence of a Gift

First, we need to ask whether giftedness from God is evident in the work of a particular composer or performer of music, poet or novelist, painter, sculptor, or filmmaker. We should ask this question about the presence of giftedness for all artists, whether Christian or not. We have already seen Calvin's thoughts about God giving gifts of grace to non-Christians. Now let us see how Abraham Kuyper applied Calvin's words in his own time:

Calvinism, on the contrary, has taught that all liberal arts are gifts which God imparts promiscuously to believers and to unbelievers. "These radiations of divine light," he wrote, "shone more brilliantly among unbelieving people than among God's saints.". . . The highest art instincts are natural gifts, and hence belong to those excellent graces which, in spite of sin, by virtue of common grace, have continued to shine in human nature; it plainly follows that art can inspire both believers and unbelievers, and that God remains sovereign to impart it, in His good pleasure, alike to heathen and to Christian. . . . This applies not only to art, but to all the natural utterances of human life.[1]

Flannery O'Connor, the great novelist, wrote about art as a divine calling and clearly believed that this calling is given by God to both believers and unbelievers:

This is first of all a matter of vocation, and a vocation is a limiting factor which extends even to the kind of material that the writer is able to apprehend imaginatively. The writer can choose what he writes about, but he cannot choose what he is able to make live, and so far as he is concerned, a living deformed character is acceptable and a dead whole one is not.[2]

There is too little space to develop this theme further here. But we should be able, I think, to express how we determine where we observe this gift for each area of the arts and in each particular form within that area. So, with Flannery O'Connor (and with the Lord) we ask, do these bones live?

Development of the God-Granted Gift

Second, we should look for the dedicated development of the artist's gift through humble learning from others, through practice, and through faithful application—in other words, through hard work as the artist lives as a good steward of the gift God has given. I see many students come through our classes at Covenant Theo-

---

[1] Abraham Kuyper, *Lectures on Calvinism* (Grand Rapids: Eerdmans, 1931), 160–61.
[2] Flannery O'Connor, *Mystery and Manners: Occasional Prose*, ed. Sally and Robert Fitzgerald (New York: Farrar, Strauss, and Giroux, 1969), 27.

logical Seminary. Some of them are extraordinarily gifted intellectually, or at languages, or at music, or at preaching. But does this giftedness lead to arrogance and laziness and dependence on these "natural abilities"? Sadly, sometimes great giftedness is treated as a source of pride and as an excuse for shoddy work.

We have all heard preachers like this, preachers who are clearly gifted speakers but who have failed to work hard at the study of their text, or neglected the necessary time for reflection on how to present their material in a manner that will communicate the truth well. Such preachers will one day have to give an account to the Lord for their failure to acknowledge their gift as a call to be good stewards of what has been bestowed on them.

What is needed, of course, is personal humility, which takes seriously the responsibility that comes with the gift. Such humility and seriousness will lead to constant hard work, eager stewardship, and a readiness to learn from others. Without these all the gifts will bear no enduring fruit. So, just as with a preacher or a doctor or a chef, we will ask whether the artist has been well trained, whether he or she has been prepared to learn from those who have mastered their discipline, and whether he or she has studied hard and applied God-given talents to the task of making "the bones live."

Service of Others in Addition to Self-Expression

Third, we should find a commitment by artists to use their gifts for others as well as for their own fulfillment. For the Christian who is an artist, the most significant other to serve will be the Lord. For a Christian working in the arts, just as for a Christian working at anything else, there should be a commitment first to offer one's gift for the glory and delight of God. Think, for example, of the movie *Chariots of Fire*, in which the Scottish track athlete Eric Liddell says, "When I run I feel God's pleasure."

There should also be the desire to use one's gift for the pleasure and enrichment of others. If either the creation of art or its performance is purely self-centered, even a great artist will not reach full potential, for God has made us to be other-centered. This will be true both for believing and for nonbelieving artists—just as for teachers, doctors, lawyers, nurses, politicians, or people working in any other branch of human activity. A Christian will also understand that every artist, both believer and unbeliever, will be seeking to express dominion over creation and to set back the consequences of the fall in order to serve the needs of other people and to bring some help, enrichment, consolation, and encouragement to their lives.

Respect for the Traditions of One's Discipline

Fourth, there will be humble submission to the rules of one's discipline, respect for its traditions, and a readiness to find freedom of expression within these forms and within the forms of God's created order. No artist ever starts from an absolutely new beginning—except for the Lord himself at the original creation. Any human artist is a sub-creator working within these creational and historical forms. With almost any work of literature or music, for example, it is immediately evident what generation and which culture the work is from—and this is as it should be; for God has not created human persons to live in isolation from one another, but rather to live as members of particular cultures and as the inheritors of unique histories. Once more, remember that I am not suggesting that the development of new forms to express one's message and one's gifts is inappropriate, but rather, I am recognizing that all artists work within artistic traditions. As in every other area of human activity, we stand on the shoulders of those who came before us and are supported by those who stand alongside us.

The Presence of Truth

Fifth, we must ask ourselves, is this work of art true? Here we come to a more difficult issue. Very few artists would question the first four points that I have made, but when one begins to speak of truth, people become wary. This is especially so in our postmodern setting, where talk of truth is seen as an attempt to impose one's views on other people. Is this another DWEM (dead white European male), or in this case another LWEM (a live white European male), insisting that everyone else think the way he does?

Let me define briefly what I mean by truth. My criterion will be very simple: Is this work of art in accord with reality?

What do I mean by this? There is a constraint on human beings in the way things are. People cannot create their own universe. Rather, both Christians and non-Christians live, reflect, and work within the universe that God has made. This is true whether they acknowledge and worship him or not. The artist is bound by the reality of what God has created and cannot inhabit any other universe, for there is no other universe. Even when a person refuses to bow before the Lord, he or she must live in the Lord's world, and so, such a person's art will have to be in touch with reality at some level, no matter what he or she may claim to believe.

Only rarely will we find art that attempts to be completely consistent with some system of radical unbelief. But art that becomes pure propaganda for a totally false universe of the artist's own making ultimately ceases to be art. Consider the example of John Cage, with his chance music, which is no longer music, but merely noise. As Francis Schaeffer pointed out, when John Cage stopped doing his "music" and lived, he had to live in the world that is actually there. Cage had a hobby of collecting and eating mushrooms and other fungi. In this hobby he was bound by the reality that some fungi are edible and some are poisonous. Cage was attentive to such boundaries in his general life, though not in his "art." But all art that is worthy of the name is bound by the glory of the reality of the world God has made and the shame of the human world as we have corrupted ourselves and fallen from that original glory.

All genuinely great art will appeal universally because of this element of truthfulness to the world as God made it and to the world of our human existence. Think of the worldwide appreciation of Shakespeare's tragedies *Hamlet* and *Macbeth*.

Consider also Jane Austen's appeal in a postmodern age; she so evidently deals with human relationships and moral questions common to all times and places that though her deeply held Christian convictions are thoroughly out of step with the beliefs and practices of our postmodern society, her novels have become increasingly popular, both in print form and in their many movie versions. Austen's work touches deep chords in the human soul because she wrote truth—truth that is immediately recognizable, even in a very different time and place.

Is There Moral Goodness?

Sixth, we need to bring any work of art before the bar of moral criteria. Again, this is a challenging issue to set forth in our moment of history. Am I demanding a new moral police force to oversee the arts? That is not my point. I am not suggesting that we can readily judge and dismiss works because they have nudity, violence, explicit sex, blasphemy, or cursing. Our judgments must learn to be wiser than those simple tests. Basically, we must be prepared to ask questions about the moral intention of the artist. Is the purpose of a work to deprave or corrupt? If a work contains immoral behavior or evil, what is the context? It should be evident to us that the Bible contains many accounts of wicked behavior, sometimes very graphically portrayed. Works of art must not necessarily be condemned because they contain such sin and violence; rather, context and intention always have to be considered.

The same is true with issues of cursing or blasphemy. It is not enough for Christians to say, "This movie or piece of literature is full of blasphemy; therefore it is immoral and we are not to see or read such works." Think about the book of Job, as an example. It is full of blasphemy, for the trite comments about God and the easy answers to the problem of suffering that Job's comforters offer him are false and ultimately dishonoring to God's name. But that does not mean that we are to censor the book of Job or to refuse to read it!

Christians can easily condemn movies or books or music that contain foul language and obvious blasphemy, but just as with the book of Job, the context and intent of the author, songwriter, or filmmaker are important. I have no wish to defend the abuse of language or the dishonoring of God's name. But before we make judgments about the way unbelievers curse and swear (in books, movies, songs, or actual life), we need to take the planks out of our own eyes.

Think about the misuse of God's name when we say, "God bless you!" and do not really mean it; or when we say, "I will pray for you," with no intention of actually doing so; or when we pretend a devotion to the Lord and a deep spirituality that is far from genuine. Think about preachers who daily on television or radio make all sorts of false promises in God's name. I suggest that such misuse of God's name and hypocrisy on the part of those who claim to know God and speak for him are far more blasphemous and much more seriously offensive to God than the open cursing in many movies and some rap music. They are also more damaging to us.

We have to consider the same sorts of issues with nudity and explicit sex. The presence of these in a work of literature, drama, film, painting, or sculpture is not by itself an indication of problems. As we noted earlier, the Song of Songs contains explicit descriptions of nudity and of very sensual sex. Yet there is no heading on the book: "For married couples only. Young people just beginning to awaken to their sexuality are forbidden to read this."

When we come across nudity and sex in any work of art, we need to ask some careful questions—and many times we will see that there is no problem. Of course we need to be aware that there are works that are pornographic in nature—either hard-core pornography or soft-core. We need to be on guard against the proliferation of pornography on the Internet in particular, for it is extraordinarily damaging to men and women and to the possibility of deep intimacy in marriage.

So, in any of the arts we need to ask, what is the moral impact of reading or viewing or listening to this piece of work? There are, of course, "artistic" works that need to be judged and found wanting—such as the pornography mentioned above. Another example of works that fail this criterion is, I suggest (though you may disagree), the novels about the cannibalistic murderer Hannibal Lecter.

I know nothing about the author, but I read one of these books when my fifteen-year-old son was asked to read it in high school. My own judgment is that there seems to be a desire to create interest in appalling wickedness for its own sake. There is some moral context, but at the same time, detailed evil is presented in such a sickening and prurient manner that it seems to me it can only damage the hearts, minds, and imaginations of those who read these works. If anyone should tell me that he or she was not corrupted in any way by reading those stories, I would be very surprised. (Interestingly, I saw one of the movies made from one of these novels, and found that it was not as troubling in this regard as the books, for the actor who plays Lecter, Anthony Hopkins, is a fine and familiar actor and he invests the character with a humanity that is absent from the portrayal of Hannibal in the novels. When we see the films, we know Hopkins already—and he, thankfully, cannot divest himself completely of his true humanity.)

Continuity of Form and Content

Seventh, we must ask questions about appropriate continuity between the form and the content of a given work of art. Is the form the artist has chosen one that works *with* or *against* the message of the piece the artist is creating? Consider Eliot's fragmented form in *The Waste Land*, a poem of disconnected pieces, disparate images, constant variations in poetic form, and a lack of rational or linear progression. This structure (or, it might be better to say, very carefully crafted lack of structure) is completely appropriate for Eliot's prophetic vision of a doomed postmodern world.

This criterion often comes into play when we hear a new song. Is the melody trite and shallow even though the words deal with profound truths or deep human emotions? If it is trite and shallow, then we may enjoy listening to the song once or twice, but we will soon tire of it, simply because of this mismatch of form and content.

Technical Excellence

Eighth, in art as in any other area of human endeavor, we need to look for technical excellence. For the Christian especially, good work faithfully done is honoring to God. Just as with a medical operation one desires to find a surgeon who is good at what he or she does and who works hard to do the surgery as well as it can be done, so too we need to be able to see that an artist has worked with diligence at his or her task. This is obvious in the arts we use in our everyday lives. Most of us want to live in houses that are well designed and well built. Most of us want furniture that is pleasant to look at and comfortable to live with. Most of us want china and cutlery that are attractive and serviceable. Most of us want clothes that look good in addition to being comfortable.

We all are constantly making judgments about the quality of workmanship and the technical excellence of the things we buy and use. This is simply part of being human. The same will be true with music, literature, painting, movies, television shows, and the like. We look for work that is well done, and we find pleasure whenever we come across what is genuinely excellent.

Integrity of the Artist

Ninth, we should have a concern for how well a work of art reflects the integrity of the artist. Is the work true to who the artist is? Or is it merely fashionable or commercial, or even false to the artist's own convictions and understanding? I am not suggesting that there is a problem with an artist getting appropriate pay for hard work; of course there is nothing wrong with writing, making music, or painting in order to earn a living. William Shakespeare and Jane Austen are examples of great writers who were very thankful to make an income from their work. Shakespeare was able to retire early because he had done so well as a dramatist, poet, actor, and part owner of the theater company for which he wrote his plays. His commercial success in no way detracts from his personal integrity as an artist.

By way of comparison, consider the challenge of preaching. It is a constant temptation for the preacher to preach what people want or expect to hear rather than what he believes deep in his heart. Sometimes proclaiming the truth according to God's Word is very difficult and is unpopular. Generally speaking, people like to be comforted and encouraged rather than challenged and convicted—and of course a preacher must proclaim truth that comforts and encourages as well as truth that challenges and convicts. Any preacher knows that some messages are difficult to hear and difficult to preach. The preacher asks his own heart: "Will people listen?

Will they fire me? Will they pay me? Will I be able to support my family?" Yet, no matter how painful these questions sometimes are, the preacher must be able to face himself in the mirror and know that he has been faithful to the Lord and to his own heart. Addressing this very issue, the apostle Paul writes: "We have renounced disgraceful, underhanded ways. We refuse to practice cunning or to tamper with God's word, but by the open statement of the truth we would commend ourselves to everyone's conscience in the sight of God" (2 Cor. 4:2). What was true of the apostle in his preaching must be true of every artist. Is there integrity in the heart as one does his or her work?

Integrity in the Work

Tenth, we should expect to see integrity in the work itself. For example, we all know that there is a difference between genuine sentiment and sentimentality. This is true in painting, in writing, in music, and in all other artistic disciplines. Does the artist seek to manipulate our emotional response by cheap tricks, or does the artist seek to generate genuine emotional response by the power of the work?

Again, preaching is a helpful example. Any experienced preacher knows how to make people cry or laugh, or how to produce many other responses through the power of the preached words. But as the apostle Paul says in the passage just quoted, preaching merely to produce an outward response is a disgraceful, underhanded way of proclaiming the message. A preacher knows when he is manipulating people, and he also knows that such manipulation will not bring about deep repentance or genuine spiritual transformation in people's lives. What is true of the preacher is also true for the composer, hymn writer, filmmaker, poet, painter, and every other artist.

Simply Entertainment!

Eleventh, we should be aware that simple entertainment is fine in almost all the art forms, for God has indeed created us to enjoy his gifts and to enjoy one another's gifts. When we watch the sun going down or pick a rose for the table, we do not need to look for anything other than the pleasure of the act itself, or the object itself. Human art, just like God's art, need not always have a "higher" purpose than enjoyment—ours and God's. Very often we will watch a movie, listen to music, read a book, or hang a painting simply because we like to do so. What matters here is the purpose or kind of art in question. Does this piece of art succeed, for me, at what it sets out to do?

The Problem of Elitism and Snobbery

There are other factors we should take into consideration in addition to objective aesthetic criteria. We need to recognize that it is not appropriate to be elitist or snobbish about other people's likes and dislikes with regard to the arts. It is fine that we all enjoy books, films, and music that are not particularly good when judged by objective aesthetic criteria. Till the end of his life, C. S. Lewis enjoyed the stories of H. Rider Haggard even though Lewis did not regard them as great literature. We all like things that are not objectively great, or even good, works of art.

In addition, we all have different tastes, and these different tastes must be respected, for this is simply an application of the command to love my neighbor as myself. My wife does not pretend to like fantasy literature, so she has never read *The Lord of the Rings*, even though it is a very great piece of literature. It would be arrogant and absurd to think less of her because of this, though I myself have read the book at least forty times. Another way to express this is to say that we must not regard artistic taste or pleasure as a moral issue or a matter of spiritual superiority. We should simply delight in the diversity of tastes, just as we delight in the diversity of personalities and areas of giftedness.

This is an important issue, and it means that we must speak with great care about the pleasures of others. We do not want to make people feel inferior because they may like a work that is not great, or even good, by objective standards of quality.

Yet There Are Objective Standards of Quality

Though we must respect people's likes and tastes, it is also essential to maintain that there are objective standards by which books, films, painting, music, or any other art should be judged. We ought to resist the "equalizing heresy" (about which Lewis wrote so well), which tells us that we must never regard some works as better than others, and that any mention of standards is necessarily elitist and snobbish.

There are standards for judging the arts, no matter how popular a given work or artist may be, just as there are standards for judging theology, no matter how popular a given thesis may be. In some cases theological weaknesses and other problems must be pointed out, and appropriate questions about the quality of the writing (or filmmaking or whatever) must be raised. No matter how carefully we pose such questions, some people will be offended and will think we are being mean-spirited, elitist, or snobbish; but this does not mean that we should be silent, though it does underline the necessity of speaking wisely, graciously, and gently.

The Devotion of the Heart

We also recognize that there is the matter of the heart. It may be that Aunt Jane, or Mr. Jones, or young Henry loves to play the piano and enjoys tapping out the music of hymns and songs of worship. Their hearts may be full of praise for the Lord as they do this, praise that he delights in and that we also should find admirable. But this does not mean that it would be wise to ask any of these persons to accompany the singing for our Sunday worship if, objectively speaking, they are not skilled or trained musicians. King David appointed leaders for music and singing who were good at their work, and so must we.

In the same way, many of us love to sing, and though we may be greatly out of tune or sound unpleasant to others, our hearts' devotion is most certainly pleasing to the Lord. But if we are tone-deaf, then out of love for our neighbors in public worship we will need to restrain ourselves from singing loudly so as not to distress tuneful ears and make it difficult for others to sing their praises to the Lord. We must have skilled and competent musicians and song leaders, but we also seek to encourage these musicians to serve the Lord in their hearts in the same way that Aunt Jane, Mr. Jones, or young Henry serve him with love.

Artistic Giftedness Is Not Equivalent to Moral Greatness

We need also to remember that artistic giftedness, even when it is great, does not make someone a better, greater, more virtuous, or more godly human being. Tolkien is a wonderful example here. He was, without doubt, the greatest scholar of the past century in his field of early Germanic languages and literature. He was also a gifted writer of stories and a thoroughly competent poet. However, he understood that these abilities and accomplishments did not, in and of themselves, make him a better or more important man in the kingdom of God. He realized that God had given him these gifts and that he was a servant who had an obligation to God to use his gifts faithfully. Tolkien knew that how God chose to use those gifts for the glory of his kingdom was God's business. Tolkien also knew that how he loved God (including the way in which he used his gifts), how he loved his wife and children, and how he behaved toward students, neighbors, colleagues, and tradesmen were the fundamental measures of his growth as a Christian—not the greatness of his gifts.

C. S. Lewis had this quality about him as well. He was a great scholar, teacher, and writer, yet he never became puffed up by the marvelous gifts God had given him. Both Lewis and Tolkien understood that they were stewards called to use their gifts wisely and well. But they also understood that what was important to the Lord was their desire to please him by living a life of justice, mercy, faithfulness, and humility in *all* they did. For Christians involved in the arts—or in anything else—there can be no higher calling.

> He has told you, O man, what is good;
>   and what does the LORD require of you
> but to do justice, and to love kindness,
>   and to walk humbly with your God. (Mic. 6:8)

5

Echoes of Eden: God's Testimony to the Truth

We turn now from our reflections about the nature of the arts to consider an issue that I think will help us understand the universal appeal of art: its echoes of the truth about the human condition. In the last chapter I suggested that one of the primary criteria for judging the value of any work of art is its truthfulness: Is this work of art true: is it in accord with the way the world is as it comes to us from God in all its beauty, as we in our rebellion have brought trouble and sorrow all over this earth and into our own lives, as we desire passionately the renewal of what is ruined and damaged? I suggested that all great art contains elements of the true story: the story of the good creation, the fallen world, and the longing for redemption.

We step back from this point for a moment to reflect on the different kinds of testimony that God has left to himself for people all across the face of this earth and all through history. Theologians have called this testimony general revelation, that is, revelation from God that comes to the whole human race, in contrast to the special revelation that comes in God's spoken declaration about himself in Scripture and through the person of Jesus Christ, the Word made flesh.

I will not write about the various kinds of general revelation in detail but will simply summarize what are usually considered the most significant forms.

Revelation through Creation

When we think about general revelation, we are accustomed to referring to God's revelation of himself in the creation around us. Psalm 19 speaks lyrically about this:

> The heavens declare the glory of God,
>   and the sky above proclaims his handiwork.
> Day to day pours out speech,
>   and night to night reveals knowledge.
> There is no speech, nor are there words,
>   whose voice is not heard.
> Their voice goes out through all the earth,
>   and their words to the ends of the world. (vv. 1–4)

In one passage Calvin calls this world a "glorious theater" in which God's glory is constantly and everywhere on display (*Institutes* 1.6.2). In the excerpt below he comments on the clarity of this revelation in the created world:

> The final goal of the blessed life, moreover, rests in the knowledge of God. Lest anyone, then, be excluded from access to happiness, he not only sowed in men's minds that seed of religion of which we have spoken but revealed himself and daily discloses himself in the whole workmanship of the universe. As a consequence, men cannot open their eyes without being compelled to see him. Indeed, his essence is incomprehensible; hence, his divineness far escapes all human perception. But upon his individual works he has engraved unmistakable marks of his glory, so clear and so prominent that even unlettered and stupid folk cannot plead the excuse of ignorance. Therefore the prophet very aptly exclaims that he is "clad with light as with a garment" [Ps. 104:2]. It is as if he said: Thereafter the Lord began to show himself in the visible splendor of his apparel, ever since in the creation of the universe he brought forth those insignia whereby he shows his glory to us, whenever and wherever we cast our gaze. Likewise, the same prophet skillfully compares the heavens, as they are stretched out, to his royal tent and says that he has laid the

beams of his chambers on the waters, has made the clouds his
chariot, rides on the wings of the wind, and that the winds
and lightning bolts are his swift messengers [Ps. 104:2–4]. And
since the glory of his power and wisdom shine more brightly
above, heaven is often called his palace [Ps. 11:4]. Yet, in the
first place, wherever you cast your eyes, there is no spot in
the universe wherein you cannot discern at least some sparks
of his glory. You cannot in one glance survey this most vast
and beautiful system of the universe, in its wide expanse,
without being completely overwhelmed by the boundless
force of its brightness. The reason why the author of the letter
to the Hebrews elegantly calls the universe the appearance of
things invisible [Heb. 11:3], is that this skillful ordering of the
universe is for us a sort of mirror in which we can contemplate
God, who is otherwise invisible. . . .

There are innumerable evidences both in heaven and on
earth that declare his wonderful wisdom; not only those more
recondite matters for the closer observation of which astronomy, medicine, and all natural science are intended, but also
those which thrust themselves upon the sight of even the most
untutored and ignorant persons, so that they cannot open their
eyes without being compelled to witness them. Indeed, men
who have either quaffed or even tasted the liberal arts penetrate
with their aid far more deeply into the secrets of the divine wisdom. Yet ignorance of them prevents no one from seeing more
than enough of God's workmanship in his creation to lead him
to break forth in admiration of the Artificer. To be sure, there
is need of art and of more exacting toil in order to investigate
the motion of the stars, to determine their assigned stations,
to measure their intervals, to note their properties. As God's
providence shows itself more explicitly when one observes
these, so the mind must rise to a somewhat higher level to look
upon his glory. Even the common folk and the most untutored,
who have been taught only by the aid of the eyes, cannot be
unaware of the excellence of divine art, for it reveals itself in
this innumerable and yet distinct and well-ordered variety of

the heavenly host. It is, accordingly, clear that there is no one to whom the Lord does not abundantly show his wisdom.[1]

Revelation in Human Persons

We see also God's revelation of himself in human nature. Because we are made in God's likeness we reveal something of the nature of God in the way we mirror his personal attributes of loving fellowship, dominion over the world, creative significance, and moral commitment. Francis Schaeffer used to call these first two kinds of revelation "the universe and its form, and the mannish-ness of man." In Psalm 8 David addresses both. He declares that God's glory far transcends the beauty of the heavens; but even though we are so little and sometimes feel insignificant, God's glory is revealed in each human person far more wonderfully than in the most spectacular sky or landscape we could ever see or imagine.

The apostle Paul seems to be referring to these two means of revelation when he says in Romans 1 and 2 that people are without excuse because they suppress a true knowledge of God and refuse to worship him. Their error is not ignorance of God, but willful blindness in the face of the clarity of God's revelation about himself. Paul appears to be saying that human nature as God's gift points up to the Creator from whom it comes, and that it is utter folly for humans to worship themselves or lesser creatures instead of the God above, in whom all glory finds its origin and home.

> For the wrath of God is revealed from heaven against all ungodli-ness and unrighteousness of men, who by their unrighteousness suppress the truth. For what can be known about God is plain to them, because God has shown it to them. For his invisible attributes, namely, his eternal power and divine nature, have been clearly perceived, ever since the creation of the world, in the things that have been made. So they are without excuse.

---

[1]John Calvin, *Institutes of the Christian Religion*, ed. John T. McNeill, trans. Ford Lewis Battles (Philadel-phia: Westminster, 1960), 1.5.1–2. In chapter 1, I quoted this passage from the Beveridge translation.

For although they knew God, they did not honor him as God or give thanks to him, but they became futile in their thinking, and their foolish hearts were darkened. Claiming to be wise, they became fools, and exchanged the glory of the immortal God for images resembling mortal man and birds and animals and creeping things.

. . . They exchanged the truth about God for a lie and worshiped and served the creature rather than the Creator, who is blessed forever! (Rom. 1:18–23, 25)

God's Revelation through Providential Care

A third form of general revelation is that God makes himself known to all peoples on the face of this earth by his providential care. This is the theme of Psalms 104 and 145 also, for in these psalms God's gracious commitment in governing all creation and his compassionate care for all he has made are celebrated. The psalmist writes:

You cause the grass to grow for the livestock
    and plants for man to cultivate,
that he may bring forth food from the earth
    and wine to gladden the heart of man,
oil to make his face shine
    and bread to strengthen man's heart. (Ps. 104:14–15)

The LORD is good to all,
    and his mercy is over all that he has made. . . .

The LORD upholds all who are falling,
    and raises up all who are bowed down. (Ps. 145:9, 14)

Jesus, also, encourages us to know of God's generous care for us when he speaks about the heavenly Father's provision for all creatures (Matt. 6:26–29), and he urges us, therefore, not to be anxious about what we eat or what we wear, or to seek after these things as the (pagan) Gentiles do, but to trust our Father and seek his kingdom and his righteousness:

> Look at the birds of the air: they do not sow or reap or store away
> in barns, and yet your heavenly Father feeds them. Are you not
> of more value than they? . . . See how the lilies of the field grow.
> They do not labor or spin. Yet I tell you that not even Solomon
> in all his splendor was dressed like one of these. (NIV)

Lest we are tempted to respond to Jesus's words by insisting that God cares only for those who are his children through faith, Jesus sets aside this thought with his assertion of how deeply committed God is to serving and caring for even his enemies. Jesus reminds us that we are called to imitate God in his care for the wicked as well as for those who obey him:

> Love your enemies and pray for those who persecute you, that
> you may be sons of your Father in heaven. He causes his sun to
> rise on the evil and the good, and sends rain on the righteous
> and the unrighteous. (Matt. 5:44–45, NIV)

> The Most High . . . is kind to the ungrateful and the evil. Be
> merciful, even as your Father is merciful. (Luke 6:35–36)

Paul appeals to this loving providential care of God when he says to the pagans in Lystra:

> We bring you good news, that you should turn from these vain
> things to a living God, who made the heaven and the earth and
> the sea and all that is in them. In past generations he allowed
> all the nations to walk in their own ways. Yet he did not leave
> himself without witness, for he did good by giving you rains
> from heaven and fruitful seasons, satisfying your hearts with
> food and gladness. (Acts 14:15–17)

God's Rule over the History of the Nations

God also makes himself known by ruling the nations in order that people might turn to him as the true source of all power and virtue. This is true when wise and equitable human government points to God as the giver of these good gifts, and it is also true when wicked rule brings disaster into people's lives and the suffering subjects turn to God for hope and deliverance. God governs history, resisting the proud pretensions of our race (as at Babel) and deposing tyrants and bringing down kings in order to draw people to himself (see the account of Nebuchadnezzar's arrogance recorded for us in the book of Daniel). In this past generation think of the overthrow of the Soviet government and the resulting open doors for the gospel to spread into many parts of the world that were formerly closed. As another example, recall the terrible massacre in Tiananmen Square, one consequence of which was that great numbers of Chinese people turned to faith in Christ.

In every kind of situation God rules history to draw people to himself and to turn them to righteousness. It should be our prayer that even the brutality of Islamic radicals will be used by God to cause many Muslims to turn sickened away from these appalling acts of terrorism and find their hope in Jesus Christ. That is what has happened under Islamic fundamentalism in Iran, with the number of Christians there growing from thirty thousand in 1979 at the time of the Islamic Revolution under Ayatollah Khomeini to over 350,000 today. Our hope as Christians is that no matter how the Devil or wicked tyrants may rage, God will rule history for the sake of the advance of the gospel of Christ.

The governance of God over the history of the nations, Paul says to the Athenians, is an evidence of God's desire to be searched for and known. He even declares that their own thinkers are aware of these truths.

> The God who made the world and everything in it, being Lord of heaven and earth, does not live in temples made by man, nor is he served by human hands, as though he needed anything, since he himself gives to all mankind life and breath and everything. And he made from one man every nation of mankind to live on all the face of the earth, having determined allotted periods and the boundaries of their dwelling place, that they should seek God, and perhaps feel their way toward him and find him. Yet he is actually not far from each one of us, for

"In him we live and move and have our being";

as even some of your own poets have said,

"For we are indeed his offspring."

Being then God's offspring, we ought not to think that the divine being is like gold or silver or stone, an image formed by the art and imagination of man. (Acts 17:24–29)

These two aspects of God's general revelation, his providential care for all people and his governing of the nations, are far less often written about or preached upon than the first two, God's eternal power apparent in creation and his personal nature made known through humans. This may be simply because almost all of us, Christians included, are so deeply influenced by the ideas of deism.

Most people believe in a god, but they think of him as a distant god who is not deeply engaged in this world or in the lives of its peoples. This neglect needs addressing in detail so that we may understand why churches are mostly silent about these two issues which Scripture speaks about with such passion and clarity. However, that is a discussion for another setting. Here I want to turn to a fifth aspect of God's making himself known to the peoples of the world.

Echoes of Eden

This fifth means of God's revelation of himself is the pool of memories within the human race of the truth about our condition: what I am calling here "echoes of Eden." It seems that among every people on the face of this earth there is recollection of the original good creation; there is awareness that the world we now live in is broken and fallen, and there is recall of the promise and hope of the restoration of what is good. This true knowledge exists sometimes in stronger form, sometimes in weaker, but is always present.

It is just as Paul says on Mars Hill to the Athenians: "He made from one man every nation of mankind to live on all the face of the earth" (Acts 17:26). We are all descended from one original human pair. Because of this common descent it should not surprise us that all people have some memory of these foundational truths about the human condition. This observation accounts, I want to suggest, for the following realities.

Echoes of Eden in Religion, Myths, and Legends

First, there are memories in religion, myths, and legends. All peoples have memories—preserved in religions and in their legends, myths, and fairy stories—of these original truths about the human situation. All over the world we find remnants of belief in one great God behind the "gods" of nature. This was true for some of the slaves brought from Africa (particularly among the Igbo people from Nigeria) and appears to help explain why so many of them came to Christian faith so quickly even though Christianity was the religion of their oppressors.

All over the world there is a sense that our present life in this world is one of having lost our way from our original dwelling place, a place that was better and more beautiful than the place in which people now live.

All over the world there is the knowledge that our present condition is one of alienation and rebellion, that we are not all we should be, that there is brokenness and tragedy in all of human life.

All over the world there is a longing for this brokenness to be set right, and there is the hope for a redeemer. Some of these elements of the biblical story are present in almost every nation's story about the past. Some contain very particular parts of the biblical account of our origins, like the almost universal existence of flood legends.

In addition there is the widespread presence of sacrifice as a means of atonement. Consider this example reported by a friend of mine who was an intermediate technology missionary in a remote part of Nepal. During his first years there he was astonished when the village celebrated its fall festival of atonement. The people took a young goat, a kid, tore it to pieces, and consumed it till none of its flesh was left. They did this to take away the sins of the community.

Or think of the legend of the altars to the unknown God cele-brated with sacrifices on Mars Hill itself. Because Paul's use of the content of legends to make the gospel of Christ known is such an interesting and challenging idea, we will look in some detail at what Paul actually does in that account so that we can understand his knowledge of his audience.

On a first reading of Paul's words in Athens (Acts 17:22–31) it is immediately obvious that there are no quotations from the Old Testament, whereas Paul's synagogue sermons—for example, the one given in Pisidian Antioch, recorded in Acts 13—are full of Old Testament quotations and allusions. His hearers in Athens were completely unfamiliar with the Old Testament, so no purpose would have been served by his assuming their knowledge of it and quoting from it, except to confuse them. Instead of quoting the Scriptures Paul quotes from two of the Athenians' own think-ers (17:28).

The first quotation, "In him we live and move and have our being," is taken from a solemn invocation to the father, and great-est, of the Greek gods, Zeus. The excerpt taken from the poem is of words spoken by Zeus's son Minos:

> They fashioned a tomb for thee, O holy and high—
> the Cretans, always liars, evil beasts, slow bellies!
> But thou art not dead; thou art risen and alive for ever,
> for in thee we live and move and have our being.

The poem Paul quotes was written by Epimenides, a wise man and poet from the island of Crete. (The second line of this passage is quoted in Titus 1:12, where Paul refers to Epimenides as a prophet.)

The second quotation, "We are his offspring," is from Aratus, the Cilician poet, and while we do not have the poem from which these words are taken, Aratus's words are very similar to those in a famous hymn to Zeus, a poem that will help us to see how Zeus was regarded by these Stoic writers:

> Most glorious of immortals, Zeus
> The many-named, almighty evermore,

Nature's great Sovereign, ruling all by law—
Hail to thee! On thee 'tis meet and right
That mortals everywhere should call.
From thee was our begetting; ours alone
Of all that live and move upon the earth
The lot to bear God's likeness.
Thee will I ever chant, thy power praise![2]

In addition to these quotations from Epimenides and Aratus, Paul begins his address by referring to the altar bearing the inscription "To the unknown god." There is a fascinating legend about the origin of this altar, and it is quite probable that Paul was familiar with the story, for the legend involves Epimenides, whom Paul quotes. If we assume that Paul knew the legend, we are helped in our appreciation of the force of his message.

We know from ancient Greek writers like Pausanias that there were such altars to unknown gods in Athens. Another author, Diogenes Laërtius, describes the legend attached to these altars. He tells how in a time of uncontrollable pestilence the Athenians sent for Epimenides the Cretan to advise them, for he was known as a man of great wisdom. He recommended the sacrifice of sheep to unknown gods, as the gods they worshipped had not answered their prayers or come to their aid. He also recommended that they set up altars commemorating these unknown gods. When they followed his advice, the pestilence came to an end, and the altars to the unknown gods who had delivered them from trouble remained on Mars Hill as an expression of the people's gratitude.

Paul's mention of the altar to an unknown God, and very probably of the legend about the altar's origin, is disturbing to some Christians. Some fear that such a reference suggests Paul's approval of pagan ignorance and worship. This is not Paul's intention. Paul is aware that the experience of all human beings is one of sorrow and trouble. Yet, when there is such sorrow and trouble, as with the plague affecting the Athenians, human beings have a sense that such disaster is not the way life ought to be. They also know

[2]Cleanthes of Assos (331–232 BC), "Hymn to Zeus."

that the only answer to their broken reality is to look to heaven for an answer—thus, the sacrifices first to the gods they worship and then, when this fails, to some other god, an unknown god who answers their prayers. Paul, of course, knows that there is one true God; but he also knows that every blessing we humans enjoy comes from the hand of this one true God. Men and women, such as the Athenians, may worship other gods (even nameless ones) and thank them for their supposed gifts, but Paul declares that every prayer that has been answered, every deliverance and good gift enjoyed, comes from the Father above, the Creator of heaven and earth. Of course God is so full of grace and kindness that he delights in answering the prayers of people who do not know him, for, as Jesus insists, he also delights in giving his good gifts to the ungrateful and to the wicked.

Paul makes exactly the same point in his words to the pagans of Lystra when they want to make sacrifices to him and Barnabas because these pagans have experienced the blessing of physical healing: "Yet he [the living God] has not left himself without testimony: He has shown kindness by giving you rain from heaven and crops in their seasons; he provides you with plenty of food and fills your hearts with joy" (Acts 14:17, NIV).

As we have seen, in our account of the third aspect of general revelation, God reveals himself by his providential care for the people of all nations. Paul knows that God is gracious to all human beings, whether they worship him or not, and God is gracious even when they mistakenly worship other gods, who are not the true God, and thank them for the blessings that come only from his hand. Even if they call these gods "unknown gods," as the Athenians did in this particular case, Paul insists that it is the God and Father of our Lord Jesus Christ who is the giver of every good gift. So Paul is quite happy to use a pagan legend as he communicates the gospel of Christ, simply because that legend has within it an element of truth or, to use our terminology here, an echo of Eden.

Many readers will be aware that Don Richardson has written extensively in his books *The Peace Child* and *Eternity in Their*

Hearts about the beliefs and practices within paganism that have echoes of truth.

Echoes of Eden in Literature

In addition to the legends that exist in the religious heritage of all peoples, there is also a stream of these memories in the literature of every nation. We might even say that all great literature addresses these issues of creation, fall, and redemption because this is the human condition, and there appears to be a racial memory of these things, or perhaps what Jung called "a collective unconscious" that recalls these deep longings and shady recollections of the true story of the origin, dilemma, and hope for our race.

But before we turn to look at echoes of Eden in literature, it is worth asking whether there are any other examples of the biblical use of legends and myths, or whether Paul's use of the legend of the altars at Mars Hill is the only biblical usage of such material.

In fact there are several interesting examples of biblical authors recognizing and utilizing such legends—legends that have an element of truth. One dramatic use of a legend comes in the highly pictorial and symbolic account of the birth of Jesus and his victory over the Serpent, recorded in one of John's visions in Revelation 12. Given how difficult this passage might appear to us, it might be helpful to have the first section of it before us:

> And a great sign appeared in heaven: a woman clothed with the sun, with the moon under her feet, and on her head a crown of twelve stars. She was pregnant and was crying out in birth pains and the agony of giving birth. And another sign appeared in heaven: behold, a great red dragon, with seven heads and ten horns, and on his heads seven diadems. His tail swept down a third of the stars of heaven and cast them to the earth. And the dragon stood before the woman who was about to give birth, so that when she bore her child he might devour it. She gave birth to a male child, one who is to rule all the nations with a rod of iron, but her child was caught up to God and to his throne, and the woman fled into the wilderness, where she has a place prepared by God. (Rev. 12:1–6; see also 12:7–10, 13–17)

If we know our Old Testaments, we will recognize the messianic title "the one who is to rule all the nations with a rod of iron" (cf. Ps. 2:9), and we might also notice the allusion to Joseph's dream of the sun, moon, and stars bowing to him; but even with these two passages in mind, John's vision still seems very strange to us. To help us in our understanding we may reflect on the way John's readers in the churches of Asia Minor would have read this text, so that we may know some of the ideas they would have had in mind as they read John's vision of heavenly portents and of the ensuing war in heaven. There are several aspects of this story that would have been familiar to John's readers from the pagan mythology widely known in their part of the world.

One of the striking elements of much pagan religion is the following story, here presented in summary. There is the hope of the birth of a divine son, a hero, or warrior. There is a declaration of enmity against this divine son and the threat of his destruction at birth. There is heavenly protection provided for the newborn infant. Then the heavenly child defeats his enemy. Versions of this story exist over much of the world in one form or another. There was one version in ancient Egypt with the goddess Isis giving birth to the sun god, Horus, after being pursued by a red dragon, Set; another in Mesopotamia with Marduk, the god of light, slaying the seven-headed dragon Tiamat. In Greece there was a particularly fascinating version of this story. Zeus, the father and greatest of the gods, begets a son with Leto. The great dragon, Python, threatens to kill the child at birth. Leto flees and is given a hiding place from Python by the sea god Poseidon. Apollo, Leto's son, is safely born and then pursues the dragon Python and slays him.

This Greco-Roman version of this common myth is the one with which all the people of the churches in Asia Minor would have been familiar. Apollo was one of the gods worshipped in the cities of western Asia Minor, so everyone would know, from childhood, the story of Python and the birth of Apollo. An interesting addition to this story is that at the time when John was writing Revelation, the Emperor Domitian demanded to be worshipped as a god and claimed in particular to be an incarnation of the god Apollo. There seems little doubt that John's readers would have recognized the myth of the birth of Apollo as they read John's vision in chapter 12 of Revelation. What are we to make of this use of a myth by the apostle John?

In his recounting of the war in heaven and the hostility of the great dragon to Christ, John is showing that Christ is indeed the fulfillment of any vestige of truth found in the myths of the pagans. Most human cultures have known that the human race has enemies in the heavenly realms, supernatural enemies who are responsible for much of the sorrow of our life in this world. Most human cultures have also had stories of the defeat of this heavenly enemy by another more powerful heavenly figure, a figure that is friendly to the human race. The story of Apollo and his birth, the enmity of the dragon, and the defeat of the dragon has within it echoes of the true story, the story of Christ.

What in the story of Apollo is just a mythical account of the defeat of the enemy of the human race is—in Christ—true history that has taken place and that has changed forever what happens both in heaven and on earth. The story of Apollo is an echo of truth, of the promise given to Adam and Eve in the garden of Eden. Christ is the reality, the historical fulfillment of that "mother of all promises," Genesis 3:15.

There is a double element in what John is doing here in Revelation 12. On the one hand, he is declaring that Christ is the fulfillment of all the best hopes and longings of paganism. He is making an apologetic point, building a bridge for communicating the gospel to pagans, using echoes of a story with which they are thoroughly familiar. Or, as Tolkien would later say, fairy stories have elements of truth, but the gospel is the greatest fairy story, because its story of the incarnation, the death, and the resurrection of the hero is true history.

However, in addition to ringing pagan bells in the ears and minds of his readers, John is also giving them a very serious challenge: Don't turn back again to the myths and stories and idols of paganism. They won't help you. They are not the truth and they have no power to save. The gods and their exploits, like Apollo being safely born, being protected in infancy, and slaying the dragon, are just stories. Christ is the reality. It is the Devil who is behind all paganism and all idolatry and behind the worship of the emperor. The Devil has been defeated, and Christ has been victorious, so don't compromise! Hold on to your faith in Christ.

Along with this pagan backdrop to the battle that John describes there is also an Old Testament background. We are told in Revelation 12:9 that the great red dragon is "that ancient serpent, who is called the devil and Satan, the deceiver of the whole world." By describing the enemy in this way John takes the heavenly battle back to Genesis 3. It is the serpent who comes to tempt the first woman and to turn her away from God to the idolatry of self-worship by his lies and deceit. Lies and deceit have always been his weapons to turn people astray from the way of truth, the way of righteousness, the way of knowing God. This liar and deceiver is the Devil, the one who himself rebelled against God and took many other angels with him in his fall (one third of them—for in the Old and New Testaments angels are sometimes referred to as "stars"). He is also Satan—that is, he is the accuser—the one who accuses believers to God, as he did with Job (see Job 1:6–12; 2:1–6) and with Joshua the high priest (Zech. 3:1–2).

What about the name "the dragon"? In the Old Testament there are several references to a monster, or dragon, known as Leviathan. As in the story of Apollo, the peoples of the ancient Near East believed that there is an enemy of gods and humans who is a serpent or dragon. Leviathan is a monster or dragon in pagan mythology, a creature that resists creation by the gods and embodies the darkness of chaos and evil. Just as John does in Revelation 12, the Old Testament refers to these myths in an apologetic way, showing the glory of the true story over against paganism. God has defeated Leviathan, the dragon, the many-headed monster of chaos and evil. God is the true ruler of his creation. See, for example, Psalm 74:13–14, a passage that refers back to the original creation and fall; and also Isaiah 27:1, a text that looks forward to the final day of the Lord, when his victory will be complete.

You, O God, are my king from of old;
  you bring salvation upon the earth.
It was you who split open the sea by your power;
  you broke the heads of the monster in the waters.
It was you who crushed the heads of Leviathan.
    (Ps. 74:13–14, NIV)

In that day,

  The LORD will punish with his sword,
    his fierce, great and powerful sword,
  Leviathan the gliding serpent,
    Leviathan the coiling serpent;
  he will slay the monster of the sea. (Isa. 27:1, NIV)

For further passages referring to this battle see also Isaiah 51:9–10; Jeremiah 51:34; and Ezekiel 29:4–5; 32:3–8. In these passages the power of Leviathan the great monster or dragon (sometimes called Rahab) is seen as being behind the power of Babylon and Egypt, the two great historical enemies of the people of God. God will slay the dragon, the monster, when he destroys the power of Nebuchadnezzar or of the pharaoh. The point of my referring to these Old Testament texts is to emphasize that the prophets used pagan mythology (in a similar way to John) to demonstrate the true power of God over all pagan religious claims.

These references demonstrate too that the peoples in the nations around Israel also thought of there being a battle with supernatural forces of evil behind the struggles that take place in this world. They too had echoes of Eden in their mythological stories. The prophets are happy to appeal to elements in these pagan myths because they knew that the myths had echoes of the truth. The pagan peoples had a hope of triumph over the enemy of heaven and earth, a hope dimly expressed in their myths. The prophets of Israel knew with certainty that the Lord of heaven and earth would defeat the heavenly enemy.

This brings us back to John's vision. In Revelation 12 John brings all these Old Testament references to the dragon, the Serpent, the Devil, and the accuser together. There is one great enemy of Christ and of his people. This enemy is the one who stands behind all the conflicts that Christians face in this world, and indeed behind all the conflicts and sorrows that all humans face in this world, for he is "the deceiver of the whole world" (Rev. 12:9).

Christians today need to be prepared to utilize these echoes of Eden wherever they are found, just as did the apostles Paul and John and the Old Testament prophets. The biblical authors used these echoes because pagan religions did indeed contain memories of the true story of our fall into sin and sorrow, our present plight under the powers of darkness, and the hope for a redeemer.

6

The Conversion of C. S. Lewis and Echoes of Eden in His Life

I have argued in our last chapter that God has been using echoes of Eden throughout history as one of his means of revealing the truth to our rebellious human race. In this chapter we turn to look at the life of one man whom the Lord reached by this means of revelation. In thinking about God's use of these echoes, I will tell a little of the history of the early life of C. S. Lewis.[1]

Longing for Eden and Discovering Joy

Since childhood Lewis had a sense of Eden, a sense that in our life in this world there is beauty, not just ordinary beauty, but beauty that lifts our eyes to heaven, beauty that is redolent of eternity, beauty that holds within it a memory of the state of perfection that was once the condition of our race.

Jack (as he was known by his family and close friends) had his first experience of beauty when he saw a miniature garden his elder brother Warnie (Warren) had made in the lid of a square biscuit tin. A child would find moss, tiny flowers, and twigs from trees and bushes with very small leaves and use these to create a miniature garden. (In rural Britain and Ireland when I was a child,

[1]The following account is my reconstruction drawn largely from Lewis's autobiographical work *Surprised by Joy: The Shape of My Early Life* (London: Harvest, 1966); also from letters he wrote to his lifelong friend Arthur Greeves, *They Stand Together: The Letters of C. S. Lewis to Arthur Greeves, 1914–1963,* ed. Walter Hooper (New York: Macmillan, 1979); also from J. R. R. Tolkien's poem to Lewis "Mythopoeia" and his essay "On Fairy Stories," published first in *Essays Presented to Charles Williams* (London: Oxford University Press, 1947), republished with some alteration in *Tree and Leaf* with the story *Leaf by Niggle* (London: Unwin, 1964).

each village had a flower show with competitions for vegetables, fruit, flower arrangements, cookery, and various home crafts. One of the classes for children was creating just such a miniature garden in the lid of a biscuit tin. I made many of these.) Lewis wrote later of the experience of seeing Warnie's miniature garden: "It was the first beauty I ever knew . . . the great bliss of Eden . . . an idea of eternity."[2]

He was six years old when this happened, and the experience was so intense that it returned to him later. He remembered it when he was walking in the garden at Little Lea, his family's second home, which was situated on the outskirts of Belfast. Something he saw caused him to recall Warnie's miniature garden, and the experience came back with the same sweetness. He wrote of this, "In a certain sense, everything else that had ever happened to me was insignificant in comparison."[3]

A second experience came from one of his favorite Beatrix Potter books, *Squirrel Nutkin*. He later wrote:

> It administered the shock, it was a trouble. It troubled me with what I can only describe as the Idea of Autumn. It sounds fantastic to say that one can be enamored of a season, but that is something like what happened; and, as before, the experience was one of intense desire. And one went back to the book, not to gratify the desire (that was impossible—how can one *possess* Autumn?) but to reawake it. And in this experience also there was the same surprise and the same sense of incalculable importance. It was something quite different from ordinary life and even from ordinary pleasure: something, as they would now say, "in another dimension."[4]

A third glimpse of beauty came to Jack through poetry.

> I had become fond of Longfellow's *Saga of King Olaf*: fond of it in a casual shallow way for its story and its vigorous rhymes. But then, and quite different from such pleasures, and like a voice

---

[2]Lewis, *Surprised by Joy*, 7.
[3]Ibid.
[4]Ibid., 16–17.

from far more distant regions, there came a moment when I idly turned the pages of the book and found the unrhymed translation of *Tegner's Drapa* and read

> I heard a voice that cried,
> Baldur the beautiful
> Is dead, is dead—
> (And through the misty air
> Passed like the mournful cry
> Of sunward sailing cranes.)

I knew nothing about Baldur, but instantly I was lifted up into huge regions of northern sky, I desired with almost sickening intensity something never to be described (except that it is cold, spacious, severe, pale and remote) and then, as in the other examples, found myself at the very same moment already falling out of that desire and wishing I were back in it.[5]

This sense of longing in him also came with the view from Little Lea, including from the front of the house a prospect of the sea; and from the garden at the back of the house the vista of the hills in the distance, the "unattainable hills." In Ireland and England the northern light is not sharp and bright and seems always to be slightly misty. This changes the colors of things in the distance and makes them blue, gold, green, and purple; the mist also makes things that are close seem far off, and things that are far off seem utterly remote. Jack had a longing to be in those distant hills, across that far ocean, but at the same time it was apparent to him that one cannot gain this place, or this experience, fully in this world.

Jack writes of these glimpses of a far-off joy that they have a similarity to happiness and pleasure, in that once one experiences the joy, one desires it again. But, he adds, this desiring repetition is where the similarity to happiness ends, for in this case it could equally be joy or sorrow that no one would trade for all the pleasures in the world. What we are calling echoes of Eden is like this, for as soon as we experience a memory of the glory of Eden,

---

[5]Ibid., 17.

there is also a sense of deep sadness intermingled with the glory, for any true echo will have both the beauty that was ours and the sorrow of its loss.

All inclinations toward God, or toward the truth of our condition, have this quality. Augustine expressed this by speaking of the restlessness of our hearts until we find our rest in God, for we are made for him and by him, but we know that we are far away from him. Ecclesiastes declares that God has set eternity in our hearts, but that we cannot find out what God has done from the beginning to the end (Eccles. 3:11). This sense of not knowing exactly what it is that one glimpses, or what one longs for, is bound up together with our memories of our true human condition: our echoes of Eden. For the truth is that we have lost our way in this world, and we do not know how to find our way home. Yet, nothing is more important to human life than these "intimations of immortality" (Wordsworth's expression).

Lewis says that this longing for God, for eternity, for he knew not what, is so important to his life, so fundamental in understanding him and what he is trying to communicate, that if we are not interested in this, then we might as well close his book *Surprised by Joy* and abandon reading it.

As a boy Jack also loved fairy stories, legends, and myths. He delighted particularly in the myths of the Norsemen, the sagas of Norway and Iceland. This began with his discovering, at about the age of twelve, the music of Richard Wagner. In the process of discovering Wagner he once again found joy.

His first encounter was a review of a translation of *Siegfried and the Twilight of the Gods*, a text of stories set to music by Wagner. A second encounter came with the illustrations for this book. Arthur Rackham was the brilliant illustrator of this text and also of a set of *Grimm's Fairy Tales*, as well as many other books exploring folklore and legends from the Germanic peoples. Rackham also illustrated Lewis Carroll's *Alice in Wonderland* and *Alice through the Looking Glass*.

Jack's third encounter was through reading a summary of the plot of Wagner's *Ring Cycle*. This delighted him so much that he wrote a poem in heroic couplets (in a style similar to Alexander Pope's translation of Homer)—an extraordinary piece of work for a boy of around thirteen. His fourth encounter was that he began listening to the music of Wagner's operas. He first heard the *Ride of the Valkyries*, then began to purchase the gramophone records of the whole *Cycle of the Ring*. His fifth encounter was seeing a full copy of *Siegfried and the Twilight of the Gods* and buying an inexpensive edition for himself.

The music of Wagner, the stories that stood behind his musical text, and the illustrations in the books that contained the stories—all these gave Jack once more the sense of joy and longing. He became fascinated with Norse mythology and read everything he could find on the subject, so much so that he became an expert on the subject in his very early teens. Joy was "an arrow shot from the north" for him from that time onward. When out walking he would look for scenes that reminded him of the caves, woods, forest clearings, and distant hills of this world of Norse mythology.

In his later writing we discover that scenes of woods, gorges, rivers, and other elements of the northern world are the ones that he is most readily able to bring to life in the way he describes and captures such landscapes for his readers. We can observe this in *Prince Caspian*, where there is a vividness to his account of the journey of the children through the overgrown and almost impenetrable woods on their way to find Aslan.

In his mid-teens Jack discovered George MacDonald (1824–1905) as a writer. Jack came across *Phantastes* at a railway station bookstall, bought it, started reading, and instantly became enraptured. He wrote to his friend Arthur Greeves of "the great literary experience" of his pleasure in reading it. This was to become the best-loved book of his life and the one that he put (in 1962) as the number-one book to shape his "vocational attitude and philosophy of life" in response to a question from *The Christian Century* magazine. Jack wrote about his discovery of *Phantastes*:

> The glorious weekend of reading was before me. Turning to the
> bookstall I picked out an Everyman in a dirty jacket, *Phantastes,*

a faerie Romance, George MacDonald. . . . That evening I began to read my new book.

The woodland journeying in that story, the ghostly enemies, the ladies both good and evil, were close enough to my habitual imagery to lure me on without the perception of a change. It was as if I were carried sleeping across the frontier, or as if I had died in the old country and could never remember how I came alive in the new. For in one sense the new country was exactly like the old. I met there all that had already charmed me in Malory, Spenser, Morris, and Yeats. But in another sense all was changed. I did not yet know (and I was long in learning) the name of the new quality, the bright shadow, that rested on the travels of Anodos. I do now. It was Holiness. For the first time the song of the sirens sounded like the voice of my mother or my nurse. Here were old wives' tales; there was nothing to be proud of in enjoying them. It was as though the voice which had called to me from the world's end were now speaking at my side. It was with me in the room, or in my own body, or behind me. If it had once eluded me by its distance, it now eluded me by proximity—something too near to see, too plain to be understood, on this side of knowledge. It seemed to have been always with me; if I could ever have turned my head quick enough I should have seized it. Now for the first time I felt that it was out of reach not because of something I could not do but because of something I could not stop doing. If I could only leave off, let go, unmake myself, it would be there. Meanwhile, in the new region all the confusions that had hitherto perplexed my search for Joy were disarmed. There was no temptation to confuse the scenes of the tale with the light that rested upon them, or to suppose that they were put forward as realities, or even to dream that if they had been realities and I could reach the woods where Anodos journeyed I should thereby come a step nearer to my desire. Yet, at the same time, never had the wind of Joy blowing through any story been less separable from the story itself. . . . That night my imagination was, in a certain sense, baptized; the rest of me, not unnaturally took longer. I had not the faintest notion what I had let myself in for by buying *Phantastes*.[6]

---

[6]Ibid., 179–81.

Lewis enjoyed MacDonald's imagination, his gift of storytelling, and the quality of "holiness" that is captured in his stories—the beauty of goodness and righteousness. Jack found holiness to be something rapturous for the first time since his early childhood. As he says, his "imagination was baptized" while reading MacDonald's story. This baptism of his imagination oriented him away from his attempts to seek orgiastic pleasure in his sexuality; away from the attractions of the occult and its forbidden, secret, and magic enticements; and back to a true and right path to joy. He was once more following God's revelation of himself through echoes of Eden.

Then, while serving in the trenches during World War I, he discovered G. K. Chesterton. When he became a young university teacher, he found the exultant psalms, and these filled him with a sense of joy and gladness. He many years afterward referred to Psalm 19 as perhaps the greatest lyric poem ever written. By the middle 1920s he began to realize that all the writings he most loved were by Christians—not just the works of MacDonald and Chesterton, but also the Anglo-Saxon *Dream of the Rood*, the medieval William Langland's *Piers Plowman*, Edmund Spenser, John Milton (in particular *Paradise Lost*, for which he was to write a famous preface), Samuel Johnson, John Donne, Sir Thomas Browne, and most especially George Herbert (who remained one of his favorite poets all through his life). Jack told himself, "Christians are wrong, but all the rest are bores!"

However, it was to be many more years before he came to a deep and personal faith in Christ. I will not give the whole account of that journey here, but will jump forward to his late twenties and early thirties, during which he was steadily being drawn toward a biblical understanding of the world and of his own life. All through these years Lewis was moving in his thinking. He had been converted to "Theism," as he says himself, not to Christianity. Even though he disliked the "collective" aspect of public worship, he had started attending worship services at the local Anglican church. He realized that he had to ask the question, "Where is religion found in its most mature expression?" He concluded that the two most "mature" religions are Christianity and Hinduism, but there were two factors that moved him toward Christianity and away from Hinduism.

One was the combination in Hinduism of, on the one hand, the philosophical meditations of a Brahmin on the divine essence, and on the other hand, just nearby, the grossest and most terrible forms of paganism with temple prostitution, the burning of widows on their husbands' funeral pyres, and other such cruelties and outright evil. The other was his own study of the Gospel records, which supported what an atheist colleague had said, during a personal discussion, about the story of the dying god having once taken place in history. As someone thoroughly familiar with literature, Lewis found it impossible to read the four Gospels as myths. They were quite clearly written as accounts of actual events. He also saw that the portrait of Jesus painted in the Gospels was thoroughly realistic. Jesus comes alive in the pages of Matthew, Mark, Luke, and John as someone who had obviously existed in history and as someone known by other people.

Consequently, Lewis had steadily moved to a position where he believed not simply in some generic God, but in that particular God who is made known to us in the Bible as the Creator of heaven and earth and as the Judge of all people. There was, on Lewis's part, intellectual assent to Christian teaching as the truth about the world. There was Jack's personal bowing before God the Creator in recognition of his own status as a creature owing God allegiance, honor, worship, and submission. There was also the humble admission of his moral failures before God the universal Judge. But there was as yet no personal trust in Jesus Christ, who is at the very heart of the truth about God, and who has dealt with the problems of our moral shortcomings by his death on the cross. Jack's mind was in one place, recognizing that Jesus had actually existed and acknowledging the historicity of his death and resurrection, but his will, his emotions, and his imagination were still far away. And in Jack's mind he simply did not understand why Jesus had come into the world, nor did he yet understand who Jesus truly was.

One night in September 1931 (the 19th, a Saturday) Lewis had a long discussion with one of his closest friends, J. R. R. Tolkien, and another friend, Hugo Dyson. The three of them were colleagues, Lewis and Tolkien at Oxford, Dyson at Reading University. Lewis said that he could not see what possible meaning Christ's life, death, and resurrection could have for him living 1900 years after the events. Tolkien replied that the gospel works in the same way that myths work. Lewis all through his life had had no problem in being moved by myths and legends. They had given him a sense of joy and touched a chord of longing in his heart. But "they are lies breathed through silver," Lewis replied. No, said Tolkien, they are not completely lies—rather, myths have a kernel of truth within the distortions and unworthy outer husk they often wear. (Here I am attempting to reconstruct their conversation from the sketchy outlines we have of it in Humphrey Carpenter's excellent biography of Tolkien, from the poem that Tolkien wrote for Jack after their very lengthy discussion, from Tolkien's wonderful essay on fairy stories, and from Lewis's own account in his letters to Arthur Greeves. The reader will understand that I have taken some license here as neither I nor anyone else alive was present on that occasion. It will be a wonderful thing one day to have these men recount the full story of their conversation that night. Any errors in this reconstruction are purely mine.)[7]

Tolkien appears to have said something like this: "Myths are echoes or memories of the truth that God had originally made known to Adam and Eve, the ancestors of the whole human race. There are in myths memories of the unfallen world, memories of Paradise, when the world was not stained by human rebellion but was characterized only by goodness and joy in all of life that belonged to God's original creation. There is also in myths a sense of the shame and tragedy of the brokenness of our present life. In addition, myths have hints of the promise and hope of redemption, of the setting right of all things." The gospel, Tolkien argued, is

---

[7]Humphrey Carpenter, *J. R. R. Tolkien: The Authorized Biography* (London: Houghton Mifflin, 1977); J. R. R. Tolkien, *Tree and Leaf* (London: HarperCollins, 2001); this volume contains the poem *Mythopoeia* and the essay "On Fairy Stories"; C. S. Lewis, *They Stand Together: The Letters of C.S. Lewis to Arthur Greeves (1914–1963)*, ed. Walter Hooper (London: Macmillan, 1979).

the true myth, the great fairy story. In the gospel of Christ all the elements of truth in the pagan myths find their fulfillment.

This conversation (which went on till 3:00 a.m.) was a very significant turning point in Lewis's conversion, for just a few days afterward Lewis came to faith in Christ. He came to acknowledge and to find joy in admitting that the truth beneath the husk of the pagan myths and legends in every culture was made sober history in the birth, life, death, and resurrection of Jesus Christ. Lewis had found the joy that had been calling him all through his life; or rather, that joy had found him.

Lewis himself would say later that what in the myths is fantastic story—story often overlaid with filth and obscenity (see his words on this subject in *Perelandra*)—is in the message of Christ sober truth that has taken place in actual history.

After that late-night conversation with Lewis, Tolkien wrote a poem called *Mythopoeia* in which he set out his views of myth, legend, and fairy story. He wrote this poem for Lewis, and he put at the head of his poem the words that Lewis had used: "For one who said that myths 'are lies breathed through silver.'" Tolkien argues in this poem that all peoples have these memories of the truth.

I will include here some particularly relevant sections of the poem. Notice Tolkien's emphasis that even though man is fallen into sin and estranged from God, yet he still has access to wisdom and knowledge from God. He still has the "rags of his lordship." Dreaming, legend making, the telling of heroic stories—these activities contain memories of the truth and of our origins as God's children. Tolkien expresses the desire that he might also be able to tell such stories—stories that, like the legends, would tell something about our true King, the Lord himself, and point people toward honoring and worshipping him. Tolkien says all this much more clearly and powerfully than my summary:

> The heart of man is not compound of lies,
> but draws some wisdom from the only Wise,
> and still recalls him. Though now long estranged,
> man is not wholly lost or wholly changed.

Dis-graced he may be, yet is not dethroned,
and keeps the rags of lordship once he owned . . . .

Whence came the wish, and whence the power to dream,
or some things fair and others ugly deem?
All wishes are not idle, nor in vain . . . .

Blessed are the legend-makers with their rhyme
of things not found within recorded time.
It is not they that have forgot the Night
or bid us flee to organized delight . . . .

I would that I might with the minstrels sing
and stir the unseen with a throbbing string. . . .

I would with the beleaguered fools be told,
that keep an inner fastness where their gold,
impure and scanty, yet they loyally bring
to mint an image blurred of distant king,
or in fantastic banners wave the sheen
heraldic emblems of a lord unseen.

A few days after this conversation Lewis finally responded fully to the truths that God had been making known to him all through his life—the truths found in echoes of Eden. From this point on Jack could finally understand why he had been so moved by that miniature garden, by the story of Squirrel Nutkin, by the verse about the "sunward sailing cranes," by the music of Wagner, by the Norse myths, by the writing of MacDonald—and by all the other memories of Eden by which God had been calling him since his early childhood.

The Birth of Narnia

Lewis never lost his interest in fairy stories and myths as vehicles of the truth. Years later he would write his own version of the story of the garden of Eden in the second volume of his adult science fiction trilogy, *Perelandra*. However, for this chapter, our primary interest is in the way Lewis undertook this same task in *The Chronicles of Narnia* and particularly in the first of these, *The Lion, the Witch and the Wardrobe.*

Though Lewis was not married until much later in life and never fathered children himself (he had two stepsons by his marriage with Joy Gresham), he was a man who loved children. Three factors seemed to have led him to become interested in writing stories for children. One was his lifelong delight in children's stories. A second was his desire to write something for the children of his friends. Yet a third was that during World War II Lewis had several children living in his home who were evacuated from London to protect them from the nightly bombings by the Luftwaffe, Hitler's air force. These children, Lewis discovered, had not known the joy of having their imaginations stimulated by good stories. They were ignorant of myths and fairy tales; they had not been read to by their parents; and they read very little themselves. So Lewis felt challenged to write for such children; he longed for them to have books that would touch their hearts and imaginations. The form he chose was the stories that became *The Chronicles of Narnia.*

Very intentionally Lewis set about to tell the Christian story in these books, but not so obviously that those who were ignorant of the Christian message would find it thrust in their faces. He wanted to capture the imagination of children and to touch their hearts just as his own imagination had been captured by the Norse myths and his own heart had been touched when he was young.

An avid student of the four Gospels, he also knew that Jesus himself told wonderful stories and that Jesus was pleased to use these stories to communicate truth to people, especially those who, for all sorts of reasons, no longer would listen to straightforward presentations of the truth. Lewis's plan was that his stories would be like the myths and fairy stories, but even more so. He would ensure that his stories were full of echoes of Eden—in particular, as Lewis said, "once Aslan had come bounding into the story!"

I need to be careful here, for I am not suggesting that Lewis's first intention was to tell the gospel story, and that he then decided to use the form of a fairy tale or fantasy to fulfill this purpose. He makes it quite clear in his own account of the origin of the Narnia stories that this is not how it happened. For him the picture of a faun walking through the snowy woods with an umbrella and Christmas parcels came first, and then the story began to develop. In the process of this development Lewis realized that this was a good form in which to communicate Christian truth. As a Christian who had the calling of being a writer, he very passionately desired to make the gospel known, but that desire was not where the story began.

Dorothy Sayers makes exactly the same point as Lewis in her wonderful essay *Are Playwrights Evangelists?* First of all, she says, playwrights are playwrights. Because they are Christians they also desire to make the gospel known, but a Christian cannot decide to write a good evangelistic play and then produce a good play. The inspiration for the play has to come first, and only later does the possibility of communicating the gospel enter the process, and even then, only if that is appropriate for the particular play that is "bubbling up" in the author's mind. Here are Lewis's own words, at some length, about the process of writing:

> All I want to use is the distinction between the author as author and the author as man, citizen, or Christian. What this comes to for me is that there are usually two reasons for writing an imaginative work, which may be called Author's reason and the Man's. If only one of these is present, then, so far as I am concerned, the book will not be written. If the first is lacking, it can't; if the second is lacking, it shouldn't.
>
> In the Author's mind there bubbles up every now and then the material for a story. For me it invariably begins with mental pictures. This ferment leads to nothing unless it is accompanied with the longing for a Form: verse or prose, short story, novel, play or what not. When these two things click you have the Author's impulse complete. It is now a thing inside him pawing to get out. He longs to see that bubbling stuff pouring into that Form as the housewife longs to see the new jam pouring into the clean jam jar. This nags him all day long and gets in the way of his work and his sleep and his meals. It's like being in love.

Lewis then writes about how "the Man" (rather than "the Author") will have to reflect on the author's idea for a book. Will it serve his purposes and the calling God has put on his life? In Lewis's case, of course, ever since his conversion, he had believed that God desired him to use his gifts to make Christian truth known, to defend it and to commend it to the world. Just as with falling in love, one has to ask whether it would be right to declare one's love and to marry a particular person. The passion itself is not enough. Lewis then turns back to his writing of fairy stories.

> Let me now apply this to my own fairy tales. Some people think that I began by asking myself how I could say something about Christianity to children; then fixed on the fairy tale as an instrument; then collected information about child psychology and decided what age-group I'd write for; then drew up a list of basic Christian truths and hammered out "allegories" to embody them. This is all pure moonshine. I couldn't write in that way at all. Everything began with images; a faun carrying an umbrella, a queen on a sledge, a magnificent lion. At first there wasn't even anything Christian about them; that element pushed itself in of its own accord. It was part of the bubbling.

Once the images had come into his mind, Lewis then reflected on the way in which fairy tale seemed the appropriate form for what he wanted to write: fairy stories are short; there is no room for lengthy description; they do not need to be about romance; they do not require a deep psychological development of character.

> On that side (as Author) I wrote fairy tales because the Fairy Tale seemed the ideal Form for the stuff I had to say.
>   Then of course the Man in me began to have his turn. I thought I saw how stories of this kind could steal past a certain inhibition which had paralysed much of my own religion in childhood. Why did one find it so hard to feel as one was told one ought to feel about God or about the sufferings of Christ? I thought the chief reason was that one was told one ought to. An obligation to feel can freeze feelings. And reverence itself did harm. The whole subject was associated with lowered voices;

almost as if it were something medical. But supposing that by casting all these things into an imaginary world, stripping them of their stained-glass and Sunday School associations, one could make them for the first time appear in their real potency? Could one not thus steal past those watchful dragons? I thought one could.

That was the Man's motive. But of course he could have done nothing if the Author had not been on the boil first.[8]

What is remarkable is just how well Lewis manages to steal past "those watchful dragons" and how deeply Christian truth is embedded into the story of Lucy, Edmund, Susan, and Peter as they journey into Narnia.

Echoes of Eden in Narnia

Where do we find these echoes of Eden in *The Lion, the Witch and the Wardrobe*?

First, we find that there are creation echoes—elements of the children's adventures in Narnia that reveal the beauty of life as it once was before deceit, betrayal, rebellion, pride, and every kind of evil entered the world.

There is the promise of new life, which is the original life, because Aslan "is on the move." Then there is the loveliness of spring, when Aslan comes and "shakes his mane." Lewis's description of the sudden coming of spring reminds us of the wonder and freshness of the original creation (which he captures so beautifully in *The Magician's Nephew*, where we read of Aslan singing creation into life). There is a memory of a more innocent time, and a happier time, in the peaceable nature of many of the creatures of Narnia. Mr. Tumnus is an example. We find a celebration of the dignity and glory of ordinary persons, like Mr. Tumnus, the beavers, and the giant Rumblebuffin. Theirs is a dignity at which we can laugh without a hint of malice but rather with glad pleasure.

---

[8]C. S. Lewis, "On Three Ways of Writing for Children," in *Essay Collection and Other Short Pieces*, ed. Lesley Walmsley (London: HarperCollins, 1991), 526–28.

There is the beauty of the snowy landscape, the frost and ice, even though this perpetual winter has been brought about by the wickedness of the witch. This beauty of perpetual winter still reveals the "dearest freshness deep down things" (words of the poet Gerard Manley Hopkins), the continuing reality that this world is made by a benevolent Creator to flourish and to be enjoyed by its creatures. Above all there is great delight in the ordinary things of life: food and drink, dancing (the fauns, dryads, and naiads), feasting (the Christmas party in the woods), marriage (the beavers), friendship, work well done, trust, loyalty, and bravery.

Second, we find many echoes of the fall—the tragedy of life as it now is. We see the reign of the White Witch: the instruments of her rule are lies, deceit, power, fear, betrayal, cruelty, sorrow, destruction, and murderous death (just as Satan's character and rule are described in the Bible). Whereas the Devil is the ruler of this present darkness in our world, in the witch's kingdom it is always winter and never Christmas. It is never Christmas because the witch hates happiness and ordinary pleasures. For her, enjoyable things are only a means to an end, and the end is always more power for her, less independence for others, and, above all, less real joy. Her fury at the Christmas feast in the woods is typical of real evil, for this is the way Satan is—he hates the good gifts of God. The witch has no love or genuine concern for anyone else. All creatures are objects to her, things to be used in her lust for power, rather than persons to be respected and honored in their uniqueness and significance.

The account of Edmund being brought under the witch's sway is masterful, for this is indeed how evil works in our hearts and minds, appealing to our worst instincts, shrewdly summing up our character flaws, and then exploiting them. She presents Edmund her treats as if they were generous gifts rather than instruments of deceit and control. The gifts of evil (the Turkish delight and the hot chocolate drink) always have a cost and do not satisfy, but rather enslave the one who receives them. Edmund begins to lie more and more and to deceive himself about the true nature of the witch, about himself, and about everyone else.

As he comes more under the witch's control, the impact on Edmund is to make him ever angrier with his brother and sisters, meaner, more spiteful, and more self-centered. All evil is like this, for it destroys our humanity, making us less than who we are. We should notice, too, that his deceit and betrayal do not make him happy, but rather more and more miserable. This is the true face of evil: it always reaps a harvest of destruction in our own lives and the lives of others. Choosing evil is a curse with many sorrows.

Indulging in evil has the effect of alienating, or separating, Edmund from others: from his brother and sisters, from the beavers, and from all decent creatures. Choosing evil has the effect of alienating Edmund from himself. His foolish choices make him very uncomfortable when Aslan is mentioned. In just this way all evil alienates us from God. Edmund's selected path has the effect of alienating him from nature and from his proper place in this world, distorting his natural and right desire for dominion, and turning it into something mean and ugly. Like all of us Edmund was intended to rule in this world as God's steward. But he becomes entranced by dreams of power. He imagines himself as king of Narnia, indulging his every whim and keeping others, especially his elder brother, Peter, in lower positions than himself. Evil has the effect of undermining his enjoyment of the beauty of creation. Just so, sin brings alienation into every area of our lives.

Yet, there is a note of hope, for Edmund is aware of what is happening in his own heart, and he is not given up fully to evil. Instead we see the struggle that takes place in him, the memories of goodness in his heart, and above all his pity for the creatures enjoying their Christmas party—the squirrels, foxes, and satyrs whom the witch turns to stone, even though Edmund intercedes on their behalf. It is this pity in him that gives us a glimmer of hope for his deliverance and restoration, for pity is at the heart of redemption—the theme to which we now turn.

Third, this story is full of echoes of redemption—the promise of what will be when Christ returns to establish his kingdom and to destroy evil entirely. "When the school term will be over and the holidays begin," then peace, righteousness, and joy will endure forever.

Aslan himself is the Son of the Emperor from over the sea. He is the Son of God, the Great Lion. He is Christ, the Lion of Judah. He is the image of Christ to us: his moral perfection and glorious power, his kingly nature and his intimate friendliness, his holiness and his gentleness, his fearsomeness and his kindness. He cannot be controlled by the children or by the inhabitants of Narnia, for his ways are sovereign and beyond their understanding. Yet just as Christ was fully human and so one of us, one to whom we can relate as a brother, so Aslan is one with the creatures of Narnia. This is brought out in a delightfully amusing way by the lion whom Aslan brings back to life and who runs around telling everyone how Aslan spoke of "us lions."

We learn of the deep magic of the penalty of death for a traitor, inscribed as law by the Emperor over the sea—a penalty that echoes the biblical teaching that the wages of our disobedience to God is death. The witch knows this magic, but has no true appreciation of the importance of justice. For her the death penalty is her means of gaining some revenge, some fulfillment of her lust for power and destruction.

At the very heart of this book we see the sacrifice of Aslan, his offering of himself as one who is innocent for one who is guilty. Lewis calls this "the even deeper magic from before the dawn of time"—the magic of his substitutionary death as he gives himself up for the traitor Edmund. In Aslan's self-sacrifice we see "justice and mercy kiss," as Lewis later was to write of the death of Christ on the cross.

We see not only Aslan's miserable death but also his glorious resurrection from the state of death. (I will never forget the first time I read this story to my two elder sons, Peter and Paul, who were then four and three years old. When I began to read about the witch and her hellish minions cutting off Aslan's mane, binding him tightly with ropes, and sharpening her stone knife—little Paul looked at me in great distress and said, "Daddy, are they going to kill him?" I said, "Yes, I'm afraid they are." The three of us began to cry; and then Paul burst out through his tears: "But he'll rise again, won't he?") Just as on that evening with my boys, whenever we read this story we join the sisters, Susan and Lucy, in their "disbelieving for joy" as they are comforted by Aslan's love and by the power of his indestructible life.

We revel in Aslan's delight in encouraging the gifts and glory of others; of giving rewards, joy, and greater responsibility to those who serve him. In the events that follow his return to life we see his healing breath giving life to the dead (the statues), and strength and courage to the weary. His defeat of the witch, the healings, the restorations to life, and the coming of spring look forward to the final renewal of all things—the firstfruits of the ultimate consummation of Aslan's kingdom. In just the same way, Christ's defeat of the Devil on the cross, Christ's miracles of healing, his raising of the dead, and his power over the created world point forward to his return and final victory over all the forces of evil and death.

In all these ways, and many more, Lewis has filled this story with echoes of Eden. Every time we read this marvelous little book (or any of the other chronicles of Narnia), we will see more of such echoes. His desire was to tell the Christian story for those who are not familiar with it, or for those who can no longer hear it because they have heard it so often that it no longer touches them.

Lewis was once asked, "Children growing up in Christian homes who are taught the gospel by their parents will recognize Christ in these stories, but what about those children who do not know the story of Christ?" Lewis responded that he hoped and prayed that children who were ignorant of the gospel of Christ would fall in love with Aslan and with the echoes of Eden throughout the Narnia books, and that later on, when they heard about Christ, they would respond to him as one whom they already knew and loved under the form of Aslan.

I have met people for whom this is true, and I am sure there are many such all over the world. With the release of the movies of *The Lion, the Witch and the Wardrobe, Prince Caspian, The Voyage of the Dawn Treader*, and, I trust, the rest of the series, it is my hope and prayer that the films' sufficient faithfulness to Lewis's story will be used by God to touch the hearts and kindle the imaginations of many, many more—and that many of these will eventually be drawn to Christ.

7

Echoes of Eden in Tolkien's *Lord of the Rings*

Blessed are the legend-makers with their rhyme. . . .

I would that I might with the minstrels sing
and stir the unseen with a throbbing string. . . .

I would with the beleaguered fools be told,
that keep an inner fastness where their gold,
impure and scanty, yet they loyally bring
to mint an image blurred of distant king,
or in fantastic banners wave the sheen
heraldic emblems of a lord unseen.

So read several lines toward the end of Tolkien's poem *Mytho-poeia*, which he wrote for C. S. Lewis after their late-night conversation that led to Lewis's coming to faith in Christ. In these nine brief lines Tolkien sets out his longing for his own career as a writer. He intends to write legends or myths, for he regards this form of storytelling as blessed, as a means used by God to make known his truth about our world and our human condition. He desires that he might write stories with poems and songs that will have something of the power of the minstrels in a medieval hall when they played their music and sang the tales of their people's heroes and their epic adventures. We can think here of the example of the great Anglo-Saxon poem *Beowulf*. Tolkien hopes to produce this kind of work with its powerful storytelling and its poetic and musical qualities.

He also desires to "stir the unseen" with the music of his words. By this expression Tolkien is communicating his eagerness to be able to write about the unseen world, the world of God and of his angels, and of the demons in opposition to him. Yet he expresses that he wishes to present this unseen world not directly, but indirectly, so that the great goodness and the terrible evil of that unseen world are revealed to the reader without an explicit account of the supernatural world being set down, and at a time before the coming of Christ.

In this, Tolkien plans for his work to be similar to the labors of the poet of *Beowulf*. That great Anglo-Saxon writer was a Christian, but he set his story in the time before the coming of Christianity to Beowulf's people. There are hints of the glory of creation, and there is the longing for redemption. But there is no explicit reference to redemption; rather there is a very powerful sense of the age-long battle against the forces of evil, represented in *Beowulf* by the monster Grendel, by Grendel's mother, and also by the dragon. In the story of *Beowulf* there is no final victory against evil, but there is heroism, courage, and the readiness to sacrifice all in the battle with the forces of darkness. Courage and self-sacrifice are, in *Beowulf*, hints or promises of the ultimate victory of faith through the coming of Christ into the world, the one who will accomplish the utter defeat of the Devil and all the hosts of darkness.

Like the *Beowulf* poet, Tolkien plans to set his stories in a time before the coming of Christ into this world. So, just as in *Beowulf*, there will be no explicitly Christian story or message, but there will be hints, hope, courage, heroism, love, and self-sacrifice in the fight against evil that characterizes the whole of our age.

In addition—and here Tolkien expresses his desires for his work as a Christian believer—he is prepared to be one of that foolish and dismissed minority of writers who offer their meager gifts to the true King of the universe, our Lord Jesus Christ. (With an allusion to Paul's words to the Corinthians, Tolkien writes of his gifts as meager, and of himself as a fool in the eyes of the world.)

In his language of bringing his scanty gifts to Christ, Tolkien pictures the magi bringing their gifts, including gold, to the King they seek, even though they know little about him. His hope is that his writing will present a blurred image of the King. This King will be distant, our view of him will be blurred, and he will be an unseen Lord, yet Tolkien's prayer is that Christ will be honored by his work. Christ will never be clearly named, but gold will be offered to him; Christ's image will be minted in all that is written; Christ's banner will be waved in every part of his stories.

This is a challenging agenda for a young writer; and it is a marvelous prayer to offer to the Lord. This hope and longing is what kept Tolkien at his work all the years of his labors on the stories of Middle-earth that make up his major completed accomplishment *The Lord of the Rings*.

In the previous chapter we looked briefly at Tolkien's view of myths. He saw them as containing memories of the truth about God, about the origin and destiny of our world, about the battle against supernatural evil that characterizes every age, and about the hope for redemption through God's intervention in human history. Myths hold within them the treasure of echoes of Eden. Myths and fairy stories are vessels containing truth—and the gospel itself is the greatest of these. Here are Tolkien's own words about the nature of fairy stories and myths. It is worth noting here that C. S. Lewis felt that his friend Tolkien, in his essay on the subject, had expressed the significance of fairy stories better than anyone else:

> The Gospels contain . . . a story of a larger kind which embraces all the essence of fairy-stories. They contain many marvels—peculiarly artistic, beautiful, and moving; "mythical" in their perfect, self-contained significance; and at the same time powerfully symbolical and allegorical; and among the marvels is the greatest and most complete conceivable eucatastrophe. The Birth of Christ is the eucatastrophe of Man's history. The Resurrection is the eucatastrophe of the story of the Incarnation. This story begins and ends in joy. It has pre-eminently the "inner consistency of reality." There is no tale ever told that man would rather find was true, and none which so many sceptical men have accepted

as true on its own merits. For the Art of it has the supremely convincing tone of Primary Art, that is, of Creation. To reject it leads either to sadness or to wrath.

It is not difficult to imagine the peculiar excitement and joy that one would feel, if any specially beautiful fairy-story were found to be "primarily" true, its narrative to be history, without thereby necessarily losing the mythical or allegorical significance that it had possessed. . . . The joy would have exactly the same quality, if not the same degree, as the joy which the "turn" in a fairy-story gives: such has the very tone of primary truth. (Otherwise its name would not be joy.) It looks forward (or backward: the direction in this regard is unimportant) to the Great Eucatastrophe. The Christian joy, the Gloria, is of the same kind; but it is pre-eminently (infinitely, if our capacity were not finite) high and joyous. Because this story is supreme; and it is true. Art has been verified. God is the Lord, of angels, and of men—and of elves. Legend and History have met and fused.[1]

Tolkien's own scholarly field of expertise was the history of the English language, in particular Middle English and Old English, or Anglo-Saxon, as well as the history of the Germanic languages. In addition to Anglo-Saxon, he was very interested in the Old Norse or Old Icelandic language and history, and he also knew Gothic, the earliest Germanic language for which we have written records. He wrote articles and textbooks and had a passion for the myths and sagas of the Germanic and Norse peoples. As Tolkien looked at the early history of English literature, he saw that there were not many myths, for these had been lost. This distressed him, and on one occasion he expressed the need for such myths for the English nation as he reflected on their existence in many other peoples:

These mythological ballads are full of that very primitive undergrowth that the literature of Europe has on the whole been steadily cutting and reducing for many centuries with different and earlier completeness among different people. . . . I would

---

[1]"On Fairy Stories" was first published in *Essays Presented to Charles Williams* (London: Oxford University Press, 1947), 83–84. *On Fairy Stories* was later published in *Tree and Leaf* (London: Unwin, 1964); a current edition is *Tree and Leaf* (London: HarperCollins, 2001).

that we had more of it left—something of the same sort that belonged to the English.[2]

Tolkien set out to do this in his legends of Middle-earth; he desired to write a myth for the English. Here we need to distinguish between myth and allegory. Some Christians have wanted to say that Tolkien's books are allegories of the gospel of Christ, but Tolkien himself rejected the notion that his books were Christian allegory. *The Lord of the Rings* is not an allegory but a myth. Rather than allegory looking back upon Christ, his stories are echoes or memories of the pre-fallen world, echoes or memories of the fall, echoes or memories of the promise of redemption and longings for the realization of these truths. These echoes are all written in the form of a mythological history of the English people and of this world. And, as was noted earlier, in Tolkien's mind the stories of Middle-earth are pre-Christian myths, hints, signs, and promises of what will one day come when the true king returns to his world to redeem it from evil.

The Origins of *The Lord of the Rings*

We have seen something of Tolkien's hope for his work as a writer, but what about the origins of the stories themselves? Where did he begin the task that would, after many years, produce this great long book with its adventures, its maps, its histories, its languages, indeed, the whole realized world of Middle-earth?

To give some background I need to go back to his years as a young boy, and I will try to summarize briefly some of the most important aspects of his education.[3] He was taught the Christian faith by his mother and followed her as a deeply committed Roman Catholic Christian from his childhood. What about his interest in languages, the languages that were to become such an important part of his life as a scholar and as a fantasy writer? Tolkien

---

[2]J. R. R. Tolkien, addressing Corpus Christi College's Sundial Society, November 22, 1914, quoted in John Garth, *Tolkien and the Great War: The Threshold of Middle-earth* (Boston: Houghton Mifflin, 2003), 52.
[3]I am drawing upon the excellent work by Humphrey Carpenter, *J. R. R. Tolkien: The Authorized Biography* (London: Houghton Mifflin, 1977), as well as my own research of Tolkien's letters and other original sources.

was fascinated by local dialect as a little child and started picking up its words; he could read by four and learned to write by five with an elegant style of flowing letters. His mother taught him at home, and he was eager to learn languages, Latin especially—he liked the sound of its words—and also French. He liked music, but for him poetry and the sounds of words took the place of music. He delighted in speaking words, in listening to them, in reading them; and, above all, he loved learning and reciting poetry. He took pleasure in drawing, especially producing pictures of trees and landscapes. His mother taught him botany, and this fascinated him. He was entranced by trees: looking at them, climbing them, drawing them, listening to the wind in them, talking to them. He was distraught when a large old willow was felled by the local miller.

Tolkien was a boy who wanted to read constantly, especially stories. Some of his favorites were *Alice in Wonderland*, tales of American Indians, the Curdie books of George MacDonald (he particularly enjoyed the goblins under the mountains), the stories of King Arthur, and the fairy books of Andrew Lang, particularly *The Red Fairy Book*. In this book is the story of Sigurd, who killed the dragon Fafnir. Tolkien wrote of this, "I desired dragons with a profound desire. Of course, I in my timid body did not wish to have them in the neighbourhood."[4] By the age of seven he was writing a story about a dragon.

By fifteen he was thoroughly familiar with Latin, Greek, French, German, and Middle English (the language of England in the years after the Norman Conquest and up till the fourteenth century). Then in grammar school (which would be high school in the United States system) he was introduced to Anglo-Saxon and loved it. He began translating *Beowulf* and other poetry; he also began to read the great Middle English poems like *Sir Gawain and the Green Knight*, *The Pearl*, and *Piers Plowman*. Tolkien also learned Old Norse, the language in which the great Icelandic sagas are written. He even studied Gothic (again, the earliest of the written Germanic languages). While still in grammar school in Birmingham he had

---

[4]Tolkien "On Fairy Stories."

mastered these languages so well that he was able to lecture and even to have spontaneous debates in them. He also became fascinated by philology, the history of languages and sound changes. He was reading widely in this field while in grammar school. His deep interest in languages and their histories led him to begin inventing languages and alphabets.

All this had become a major part of his life before leaving school, so where would this interest in languages, medieval stories, and the history of languages take him during his college years? By eighteen he was writing poetry about fairies and elves. Then he discovered the great Finnish poem *The Kalevala* and learned Finnish to read it in the original. On the basis of that language he began to create Quenya, which would later become the language of the High Elves. He also learned Welsh and developed his skill in painting and drawing, as well as in handwriting and calligraphy. He had begun to study the classics, Greek, and Latin at Oxford, but he changed his course from classics to English, especially the ancient and medieval languages that lie behind modern English.

Of particular importance was his discovery of the Anglo-Saxon poem *Christ* by Cynewulf. Two lines from this became the inspiration for part of his conception of Middle-earth:

Hail Earendel, brightest of angels
above the middle-earth sent to men.

These lines pleased him so deeply that he wrote a poem about Earendel. He also came across the works of William Morris and particularly enjoyed his *House of the Wulflings*.

He carried on working on Quenya and then began to create another language, Sindarin, this time modeled on Welsh. He recognized that this labor on his new languages was "a mad hobby." (These languages are developed to the point that anyone can actually learn them, speak them, and write them.)

A turning point came when Tolkien realized that if one is going to create a language, then ones needs people to speak it. He decided that elves who were seen by Earendel on his voyage across the heavens were to be the speakers of his languages. He began to write poems about some of these elves and the humans that they encountered. Then he felt that these elves and men needed a history. The final addition was a world in which these characters dwelled and had their adventures.

Right up until the end of Tolkien's life he carried on writing the history of Middle-earth. One of the fascinating things about *The Lord of the Rings* is that there is such a rich background to everything said in it. Tolkien produced maps, family trees of all his characters going back many generations, poems, songs, legends, philological notes on the languages, and histories of those languages.

This is a very simplified account of the origins of Tolkien's history of Middle-earth and some of its characters. You may wonder, "Surely, these books about hobbits, elves, dwarves, and men are first of all stories, just stories, are they not?" Indeed they are stories and Tolkien delighted in stories. In the early 1930s, Tolkien started telling stories to his four children. He was a wonderful storyteller. Many of his published stories find their origin in tales that he would tell his children. Some of the first stories he told his children were about Bilbo Baggins, the hobbit.

This question about whether the books are just stories raises the issue of why *The Lord of the Rings* has been so extraordinarily popular, and why the films made with great respect for the books have been such a success. A discussion of the reasons for the popularity of the book and movies will bring us back to the matter of myths and fairy stories.

Why Such Popularity?

So why do people enjoy these books so much? Why are books published in the 1950s creating such a stir today? Even before the release of the movies there were more than fifty million copies of *The Lord of the Rings* in print. Today, after the huge success of the movies, even the publishers are hesitant to give figures for the overall sales of *The Lord of the Rings*. Besides the various editions of the book in English, there are translations into many languages.

The movies won a record number of Oscars and have been seen all over the world by many millions of people. Recall my recounting earlier how at the turn of the millennium Tolkien was declared the author of the century. He won this hands down over James Joyce and Virginia Woolf, the authors that the scholars and critics doing the poll wanted to win; in fact the pollsters were so unhappy that Tolkien won easily, they did their poll a second time hoping for a different result, but to no avail. In a poll conducted by BBC television *The Lord of the Rings* was voted the best-loved book of the British people. So, what are the reasons for this remarkable success?

The Stories

These books have achieved such popularity, in part, because Tolkien is a great storyteller who captures the reader's imagination very quickly. Donald Barr, a professor at Columbia, puts it this way: "It is an extraordinary work—pure excitement, unencumbered narrative, moral warmth, barefaced rejoicing in beauty, but excitement most of all; yet a serious and scrupulous fiction, nothing cozy, no little visits to one's childhood."[5]

The compelling nature of the story is also one of the reasons why this book has made such enjoyable films. *The Lord of the Rings* movie trilogy is filled with exciting events and situations that lead you to wonder how on earth the characters are going to get through. A reader or moviegoer can experience wonder and suspense again and again through these stories even though he or she knows exactly what is going to happen. That is one of the marks of a well-told story. Though I have read the book many times, I still get caught up in the story every time, and I have to tell myself to slow down so that I do not miss details of the text or the quality of the writing.

The Writing

Second, these books are beautifully written. There are no wasted words. Tolkien wrote and rewrote his stories and poems. He would

---

[5]Donald Barr, "Shadowy World of Men and Hobbits," review of *The Two Towers, New York Times,* May 1, 1955, accessed, www.nytimes.com/1955/05/01/books/tolkien-towers.html?_r=0.

send bits and pieces to close friends like C. S. Lewis. Lewis made his comments, and even when the comments were almost entirely positive, if there were any sort of editorial suggestions or hesitancy about any aspect of what was written, Tolkien would rewrite the whole segment over and over again. Every single word adds to the picture we are given.

One test for determining whether something is well written is to hear it read aloud, either in a professional recording or by a friend or family member. I first became acquainted with Tolkien's books when my father read them to my brother and me after they were initially published in England. For months we were occupied getting through these books. Since then I have read the books over and over for both my own enjoyment and the enjoyment of our children and now our grandchildren. A book that is not well written, no matter how compelling the story is, will not be reread multiple times. I know people who reread *The Lord of the Rings* every year. Christopher Lee, the actor who plays Saruman the Wizard in the movies, says he reads the books once a year. And like many, Lee is able to enter into and enjoy Tolkien's Middle-earth again and again.

The Characters

The Lord of the Rings story is captivating because of the characters we meet. There are hundreds of characters who are part of the history of Middle-earth. Essential to the value of this literature is the fact that amid many lesser characters, the main characters are developed with real depth. People like Bilbo, Frodo, Sam, Gandalf, and Aragorn are thoroughly realized people. You can imagine yourself having a conversation with them. They become known individuals through this story, and that, of course, was one of the real challenges for the filmmakers. They were faced with the problem of not wishing to offend the great numbers of people who were already familiar with the characters through the books. But they were also at an advantage because the characters in the books are so well developed, and the director and the actors had something solid with which to work.

The Place

A fourth reason why people fall under the "spell" of Middle-earth is that Middle-earth itself is so thoroughly realized. Every sentence in this three-lengthy-book set (there are actually six sections to the work as it was written) is related to a vast story that stands behind it. Everything mentioned contributes in some little way to this extraordinarily intricate story. That is one of the most remarkable and engaging aspects of these books. Today there are Tolkien societies and Middle-earth societies made up of people who do such things as learn Quenya and Sindarin and write letters to each other in Tolkien's two elvish languages.

The Realism

It is interesting to use the word realism in relation to books that are fantasies. But people constantly try to relate what takes place in *The Lord of the Rings* to events in the modern world. I have read reviews that see the movies as a commentary on the war on terrorism today. When the books were first published in the 1950s, many people saw them as a commentary on the rise of Hitler and the Nazis in Europe, and the events of World War II, or the rise of communism in the Soviet Union and Eastern Europe, or the development of the atomic bomb.

Tolkien always denied that his books had anything to do with the World Wars, or the Cold War, or nuclear weapons, though he himself had experienced some of the appalling events of World War I in Europe. Several of his close friends were killed in the war in France; he saw the death of great numbers of his fellow soldiers in the Battle of the Somme; and he himself was invalided out of the Somme with trench fever. Even though Tolkien denied that his books were about these great wars, and we may deny that these books are about the present-day terrorist crisis, the books are so realistic in their depiction of human life that they touch us all at a very deep level—because they most certainly are about the ongoing conflict with terrible evil—evil that takes a slightly different form in every generation. This is another major reason why people immediately flocked to the movies and love the books. Whatever evil we encounter, we see its face depicted clearly in *The Lord of the Rings*.

Flannery O'Connor wrote some fascinating words in *Mystery and Manners* that relate to this point of realism. She says, "I'm always highly irritated by people who imply that writing fiction is an escape from reality. It is a plunge into reality."[6] Those words are very appropriate as a description of Tolkien's books. They are a plunge into reality, even though they are fiction, even though they are fantasies about a completely imaginary world. Lewis explains this irony in a review of *The Lord of the Rings*:

> "But why," (some ask) "why, if you have a serious comment to make on the real life of men, must you do it by talking about a phantasmagoric never-never land of your own?" Because, I take it, one of the main things the author wants to say is that the real life of men is that mythical and heroic quality. . . . The imagined beings have their insides on the outside; they are visible souls. And Man as a whole, Man pitted against the universe, have we seen him at all till we see that he is like a hero in a fairy tale?[7]

Lewis's point is simply that we learn about who we really are by reading stories. That is the quality that attracts so many millions of people to Tolkien. Yes, he is a great storyteller, but there is something operating at a very much deeper level. People recognize the struggles and happiness of the human condition, the sorrows and joys of all our lives, in these stories. No doubt, that is the fundamental reason for their popularity, and this brings us back to Tolkien's view of legends and fairy stories—that they contain echoes of Eden, memories of the truth of our human situation.

In the case of *The Lord of the Rings* Tolkien has very purposefully rooted the stories in a true account of the human condition, of our brokenness. There is a kind of terrible, sober realism about what Galadriel calls "fighting the long defeat" against evil. The

---

[6]Flannery O'Connor, *Mystery and Manners: Occasional Prose*, ed. Sally Fitzgerald and Robert Fitzgerald (New York: Farrar, Strauss, & Giroux, 1970), 77–78.
[7]C. S. Lewis, "A Review of J. R. R. Tolkien's *Lord of the Rings*," in *Essay Collection and Other Short Pieces*, ed. Lesley Walmsley (London: HarperCollins, 1991), 524–25.

truth is that every one of us is going to die. We fight a long defeat against evil until the last enemy, death, takes us; and it will only be at Christ's coming that this last enemy is destroyed. That is the reality of the human condition, and this comes out so powerfully in Tolkien's books.

Elsewhere Aragorn says that there are sorrows in our lives so great that the tears cannot be wiped away in this world. This is the grim reality of daily existence, a reality that will not change until Christ himself wipes away our tears. Readers (and moviegoers) are drawn to the realism of the myth that lies within and behind the story.

The Myth

As we think about this realism, many people acknowledge that the story is a plunge into reality that is informed by Germanic and Norse myths and sagas. In fact, a review of the first film said that these books have nothing to do with Christianity, but are purely about Germanic and Norse sagas. It is certainly true that the books are influenced greatly by Germanic and Norse myths and sagas. But they are much more deeply influenced by a Christian account of the world. The stories reflect the Bible's account of creation, the fall of humanity due to rebellion against God, and the redemption that God will accomplish.

Commentators who are antagonistic toward Christianity recognize this Christian background to *The Lord of the Rings*. I have read several interviews with Phillip Pullman, who has written his own fantasy works. He says that one of the reasons for his writing is that he is fed up with the Christian impact of Tolkien and C. S. Lewis.[8] Other passionate humanists have said they hate Tolkien and Lewis, whom they see as "riding in on a white horse," trying to rescue civilization by turning people back to the Christian faith.

Despite this recognition, by enemies of Christianity, of the deep influence of the Christian faith on Tolkien's book, W. C. Dowling

---

[8]Interview with Philip Pullman, "The Art of Darkness," *Intelligent Life*, December 3, 2007; there are many such interviews with Pullman in which he has made disparaging criticisms of the works of Lewis and Tolkien.

says that these books contain "no trace of religious belief, ritual, or theology."[9] Dowling questions how a narrative that demands that readers conceive of the world within religious categories can do so without any overt mention of religion. This brings us back to the issue of allegory. When the books first came out, and for years afterward, many people thought of *The Lord of the Rings* and the stories of Middle-earth as an elaborate Christian allegory. But as I mentioned earlier, Tolkien himself denied that they were a Christian allegory. He wrote to his publishers saying, *"The Lord of the Rings* and *The Hobbit* is not about anything but itself. Certainly it has no allegorical intentions, general, particular, or topical, moral, religious, or political."*[10]

Tolkien said he personally was not interested in writing allegories, and that he had no intention of being didactic, that is, teaching certain moral standards or values as he wrote *The Lord of the Rings*. He insisted that his books are just stories. They are indeed just stories, but they are stories that reflect truth. Tolkien specifically regarded them as fairy stories. And it is important to understand what Tolkien said about fairy stories. He believed that there can be far more truth revealed in a fairy story or in a myth than in a realistic novel. That Tolkien thought of them as fairy stories or myths does not in any way mean that he thought of them as being less serious in what they were communicating. Remember the words from *Mythopoeia* at the head of this chapter. Tolkien's desire was to sing the story of the one true king and his good creation, of our rebellion against him, and of his commitment to defeat our enemies and to win us back from our rebel state.

In *The Lord of the Rings* there is indeed no mention of religion, the Bible, the church, Christ, the sacraments, or worship rituals—but *the unseen and unheard backdrop to every moment of* The Lord of the Rings *is the biblical story*. It is the story of the battle between light and darkness, between good and evil; the story about the coming of the kingdom; the story of a good creation that has been given to

[9]W. C. Dowling, course description of "English 321: Tolkien and Oxford Christianity" (Department of English, Rutgers University), accessed, http://www.rci.rutgers.edu/~wcd/tolkien.htm.
[10]Philip Norman, "The Prevalence of Hobbits," interview, *New York Times*, January 15, 1967, accessed, http://www.nytimes.com/1967/01/15/books/tolkien-interview.html.

the inhabitants of the world; the story of the marring and falling of that world into disobedience, evil, and death; the story of the hope of the restoration of what is good, and the redemption that brings that restoration about. Yet, God is explicitly mentioned only once (and then only in some editions of the book)—when Gandalf is fighting the Balrog at the bridge in Moria, just before he plunges into the abyss to destroy the Balrog while giving up his own life.

Yet, despite the Creator and Sustainer of the universe being rarely if ever named, God is always present—God invisibly at work fulfilling his purposes in the world through his divine providence and sovereign rule over history. If you read the book with care, the "distant king" is constantly on his throne wisely and graciously governing the events of the story—even though he is unseen and unheard.

There is the memory of Paradise as it originally was—the constant echo of the good creation. We see this at the most basic level of a delight in the daily providence of a good God and his gifts of common grace. Particularly among the hobbits there is the delighted enjoyment of the ordinary gifts of life—food, drink, laughter, work, home, presents, parties, and fireworks! This element of joy in the goodness of creation is also present among the elves as a natural part of their lives, and among all the humans who are decent people.

The books are full of the love of creation and reveal, among the good characters, a wise, careful, and just exercise of dominion. Think of the way the elves Celeborn and Galadriel have built their city among the trees in Lothlórien; or of the city of Rivendell, the "last homely house," and the glorious stone architecture of Elrond's palace; or of the manner in which the dwarves bring the inherent glory out of stone and jewels in underground caverns; or of the beauty of the Shire and the way the homes of the hobbits and their care for the land is like a memory of the garden of Eden.

There is a lovely realization of joy in human relationships between family members and friends, a celebration of tenderness between people, of faithfulness and loyalty, and of genuine goodness and service to one another and self-sacrifice. Tolkien expresses love without any sentimentality, kitsch, or shallowness.

It is extraordinarily difficult to write well about goodness. Lewis makes that point in his introduction to *The Screwtape Letters*. While it is actually quite easy to write about evil, it is much more difficult to write about goodness and make it seem real. Incidentally, this is one of the lovely things about the Gospels; Jesus is shown to be perfect but he is real, and the story has the ring of truth about it. Tolkien works at that level too, constantly communicating a happy realism in the goodness and the joys of human existence.

Interestingly, and sadly, in the movies this quality of goodness comes over much better when the glory of creation is shown than when people are present on the screen. For example, viewers have said that they do not think the holiness or goodness of the elves is very well realized in the movies. This is particularly so in scenes with Galadriel or Elrond, for we recognize that these scenes do not convey the kind of deep holiness and goodness of the elves that is expressed in the books. The director and cameramen use light, stillness, and physical beauty in their attempt to present moral beauty, just as Tolkien does in his text, but because their actors are fallen human persons, it is impossible for them to shine with the radiance of moral glory that is present in Tolkien's characters.

If we ask why it is so difficult to communicate genuine holiness visually, I think it is because we are so unfamiliar with perfection ourselves. None of us has a heart without deception and all kinds of ugliness and pride. Consequently, it is perhaps an impossible task for an actor to portray a person who is thoroughly and completely good. Representing moral perfection in visual form is extraordinarily difficult to do. It is so alien to our experience that it may be impossible until we ourselves are made whole by the Lord.

There is also the loss of Paradise and the sad reality of the present fallen world—this too is at the heart of the story. Tolkien has written a fairy story that laments the destructive nature of evil. Behind the evil we see the satanic figure of Sauron and his hellish servants. There are other ancient powers of evil like the Balrog who dwells deep in the mines of Moria, or Shelob hiding in her lair beside the path into the desolate land of the dark lord. Tolkien, faithful to Scripture, presents these powers of evil without any trace of goodness. There is nothing to admire about them, for they are given up entirely to evil. They are darkness without any light.

When we look at the other characters, we see in them the battle between good and evil and the way each person's choices set that person's destiny and his or her impact on others for good or ill. Think of the choices that Sam has to make, or Boromir, or Gimli, or Aragorn, or even Gollum, who is not yet so utterly lost that we cannot see the slightest glimmer of the possibility of his redemption.

Many of the characters face the temptation of power (symbolized especially by the Ring itself). We may think here of the wrestling with the false promises of power faced by Galadriel, by Sam, or by Boromir. We also meet those who give themselves up completely to this temptation, like Saruman; and then we lament the terrible corrupting nature of power when it is used for its own ends. Tolkien knows that the wages of sin is death, and that anyone who sins becomes a slave of sin. Saruman and Wormtongue are shocking examples of the enslaving nature of sin and of the way that sin so miserably reduces the humanity and glory of those who give themselves up to it. They become shadows of themselves.

There is the hope of redemption and the regaining of Paradise—the book is shot through with echoes of the story of our salvation. We will look first at the virtues that are celebrated in the story, for this is one of the qualities that make *The Lord of the Rings* such an inspiring book. The virtues most treasured in the stories are those at the very heart of the Christian gospel. Just a few illustrations of this will reveal how thoroughly these qualities are woven into Tolkien's work.

The first we may consider is *meekness* and *humility*. It is no accident that the heroes of *The Lord of the Rings* are hobbits—that is, halflings. Hobbits are little people, just three to four feet tall. Most of the people in the world outside their home, the Shire, do not even know they exist. Yet these "weak little" people are at the center of the great events that bring about the overcoming of evil. There is a wonderful statement in *The Fellowship of the Ring* by Elrond, one of the great leaders of the elves:

> The road must be trod, but it will be very hard. . . . Neither strength nor wisdom will carry us far upon it. This quest may be attempted by the weak with as much hope as the strong, yet such is oft the course of deeds that move the wheels of the world. Small hands do them because they must, while the eyes of the great are elsewhere.[11]

The hobbits' quest to destroy the Ring is like a commentary on Paul's words in 1 Corinthians about God using the weak and foolish things of the world, and the things that are not, to destroy the wise and mighty things of the world, the things that are. The story is also like an exposition of Jesus's words in the Sermon on the Mount: "Blessed are the meek, for they shall inherit the earth" (Matt. 5:5). The virtue of meekness is at the very heart of *The Lord of the Rings*. The heroes of this story are meek people who do not want power. They are interested in what is good and true, no matter what it costs them. Francis Schaeffer used to say, "There are no little people in God's world." In fact, little people are all extraordinarily significant and that is, of course, the point that Tolkien is making in these stories.

A second and very closely related virtue, one central to this story, is *service to others* without desire for recognition or fame. A fascinating example of this is shown in Strider, or Aragorn, who is basically unknown and unappreciated and has no interest in being known. The appendices at the back of *The Return of the King* tell us that Aragorn has already spent decades working as a soldier and senior military leader and advisor to the Rohirrim in Rohan and also in Gondor. In both places he fades out of the picture because he has no desire to be recognized or to have power. Of course Aragorn becomes the king in the end (King Elessar). But he spends many decades living in anonymity and many ignorant people assume that he is some sort of rogue, while in truth he is a ranger who gives his life without praise or reward defending the hobbits' homeland, the Shire, (and other places) against the evils growing in Middle-earth.

---

[11]J. R. R. Tolkien, *The Fellowship of the Ring* (New York: Ballantine, 1965), 302.

A third virtue displayed in the stories is *self-sacrifice.* Self-sacrifice is, of course, at the heart of Christianity—particularly the sacrifice of Christ. And self-sacrifice is at the center of *The Lord of the Rings.* Whether it is Gandalf, prepared to sacrifice himself in Moria, or Theoden going out to battle, knowing he is going to die, repeatedly the central characters are willing to give up their lives out of love for others. Aragorn, the servant king, faces the possibility of death countless times in his commitment to love and serve others. Frodo and Sam go to Mount Doom with no hope of surviving, but ready to sacrifice themselves for the salvation of others. Galadriel says, "Together through the ages of the world we have fought the long defeat,"[12] and she knows that she and the rest of the elves must diminish if evil is to be defeated and others are to be delivered from its power.

Yet this story also gives us foretastes of redemption. As already mentioned there are hints of a divine providence turning history toward hope—indeed the hidden hand of God behind the story is the most vivid presence and the most powerful force in the overcoming of evil. We also see brief pictures of Christ's glory in Gandalf's fight with the Balrog in Moria and his plunge into the abyss and death as he defeats his enemy; in the resurrection of Gandalf and his transfigured appearance to Aragorn, Legolas, and Gimli when they meet him in the forest of Fangorn; and when Gandalf appears at the climax of the Battle for Helm's Deep as the rider on a white horse wielding his sword and overwhelming the evil armies with light and majesty. We also see glimpses of Christ in the character and life of Aragorn, the servant king, and his eventual return to Gondor to take his place on the throne of his ancestors.

Finally there are quiet intimations of immortality. Think of Sam's vision of the star, which fills him with the hope of goodness and beauty that will never be destroyed or lost; or of the last journey of Frodo across the sea to his healing and the sight of a swift sunrise.

---

[12]Ibid., 400.

Such echoes of Eden cause people to respond at a deeper level than they themselves realize when they read *The Lord of the Rings* or see the movies. I have no doubt that it is not just the great filmmaking, the technological wizardry, the excellent characterization, the marvelous story, the remarkably realized world of Middle-earth, the journey of the quest, or any of the other great literary qualities of *The Lord of the Rings* that makes these books and films so popular. Working in and through these qualities, it is the echoes of Eden and the longing for redemption that touch people deep within the hidden recesses of their hearts. Paradise once owned, paradise lost, and paradise that might be regained—these are the memories and longings present in every moment of the story. They are the truths hidden in every heart (often intentionally suppressed), and they speak to every reader of the books and every viewer of the films.

8

Harry Potter and the Triumph of Self-Sacrificing Love

The Harry Potter books are an extraordinary success story in the publishing world. Over the past few years they have aroused much interest and excitement not only in the original English language editions, but also around the world as they have been translated into many other languages. Their translation into Chinese was reported to be the biggest publishing event in China's history. The Harry Potter books strike a chord with both children and adults, and the Harry Potter movies have been released to packed theaters. The fourth book in the series had an initial print run in the United States of 3.8 million copies, forty times as many as an average bestseller. The final film, the second part of *Harry Potter and the Deathly Hallows*, released in 2011, has broken box office records. What are we to think of this remarkable publishing and filmmaking success?

At the most practical level, as well as being extraordinarily popular, the books have encouraged millions of children to start reading for the first time. Many parents are delighted to see their children eagerly reading these stories and then moving on to read many other books.

For readers of this book I hardly need to point out that there have been many passionate attacks on the Harry Potter series, in particular by Christians. This has occurred especially in the United States—much more than in Britain or other places. In the States, Christians on the radio, in magazine articles, on television, on websites, and in a growing number of books have attacked this series very strongly. Some Christian schools have banned the books. I have had several telephone calls, letters, e-mails, and face-to-face questions from confused parents saying, "My children love these books, I love these books—what is going on?"

Criticisms of the Harry Potter Books

What are the criticisms that have been leveled at the books and their author, J. K. Rowling?

First, the strongest criticism has come because the books bring readers into an imaginary world of magic and wizards; and therefore, many Christians say that it is abundantly clear that the books offend against the biblical condemnation of witchcraft and wizardry. These critics insist that because Satan is behind all witchcraft and wizardry, Rowling's books most certainly teach occult practice to their young readers.

Second, many Christians simply say that fantasy is dangerous, and that to present this kind of fantasy or magical world to children is automatically hazardous to them. This objection builds on the first attack on the books, for these critics insist that fantasy is a close relative of the occult.

Third, an additional criticism charged against these stories is that the books teach a rebellious attitude toward authority. To support this attack critics cite the way Harry sometimes responds to his uncle and aunt who are raising him. The argument goes that Harry's reaction to Uncle Vernon and Aunt Petunia are proof of his insubordinate mentality, and therefore children reading the books will be encouraged to be rude and disobedient to their parents or to others in authority over them. I will respond to this criticism immediately here, for anyone who has read the stories with any sympathy needs to admit that Harry's uncle and aunt are some of the most unpleasant people one can imagine. They treat Harry very poorly to say the least. To put the truth a little more bluntly, they are abominably cruel guardians. As a small child Harry is given a tiny cupboard under the stairs without windows or light as his room. He is inadequately fed, while his aunt and uncle stuff their own son, Harry's cousin Dudley, with food and spoil him in every conceivable way. As a consequence of this poor parenting, Dudley becomes as fat as a pig and thoroughly self-centered. He is often cruel to Harry in imitation of his father and mother, Harry's uncle and aunt. The uncle and aunt treat Harry much worse than most people treat the most neglected servant. My own view is that most of the time Harry behaves with extraordinary restraint toward two of the wickedest relatives that one could imagine. In any righteous society Uncle Vernon and Aunt Petunia would be imprisoned for child abuse of the very worst kind. I have to say that I believe this criticism of the books to be absurd.

The view that the books encourage occult practice—with the charge often added that Rowling is a witch herself—is a very serious accusation to make against an author. It should be noted here that some Christians make the same accusation against C. S. Lewis and J. R. R. Tolkien for two reasons: first, there is witchcraft, wizardry, and the practice of magic both in the Narnia series and in *The Lord of the Rings*; second, these books by Lewis and Tolkien are fantasies, and, once again, the charge is made that fantasy leads children to the occult. This of course is a very serious accusation to make against these two authors, both of whom are generally recognized to have been devout Christian believers. However, there are many Christians who hold this critical view very strongly. Because I have publicly defended the Harry Potter books, as well as the books of Lewis and Tolkien, I myself have been publicly condemned in these words: "You, Jerram Barrs, will burn in the lake of fire together with J. K. Rowling, C. S. Lewis, and J. R. R. Tolkien."

Before I respond to the first two major criticisms (and they are really one), let me set out very briefly why I like the books so much. In giving my reasons for enjoying the books I will, of course, begin to answer the charges that have been made against them and against Rowling herself.

Why I Like the Harry Potter Books

1. The seven Harry Potter books are great fun to read. Consider, for example, the game of Quidditch, in which the players fly on broom-

sticks and have to be constantly watching for all sorts of different challenges. I will not give a fuller account of the aerial contest, but simply say that I find the descriptions of the game captivating. At times when I am reading, I will laugh out loud from pleasure and amusement. An example comes in the last book, with the escape of Harry, Hermione, and Ron from the Wizard Bank of Gringotts on the back of a blind dragon. There are many such happy moments in the reading of these books, and this element of fun is one of the reasons that children (and adults) enjoy the books so greatly.

2. Rowling has created a delightful world of the imagination. She has constructed an alternative universe, another dimension (rather like Lewis's Narnia or Tolkien's Middle-earth), but Rowling's alternative universe is right alongside and, for much of the time, right within our world. The children catch a train at King's Cross Station (notice the name King's Cross—certainly not selected accidentally, and in the very last volume it becomes very clear why Rowling chose such a name). King's Cross station is in London, of course, and platform 9 3/4 is invisible to ordinary people (Muggles). The students head off in a beautiful old steam train to their school Hogwarts where they will learn to be witches and wizards. This other world of wizards and their family and social life is thoroughly realized and consistent with itself—just as Narnia and Middle-earth are thoroughly realized and inwardly consistent. This is, I believe, a challenging task for an author, and I think Rowling has succeeded remarkably well.

Of course, it is this alternative universe of the imagination that leads to the charge of the danger of fantasy. I will return to this charge later, though I simply point out here that those who have a problem with the idea of fantasy and alternative universes need to recognize that almost all children play imaginative games in their minds, starting at a very young age. I should also add that little children have no difficulty whatsoever in distinguishing between their imaginary world and reality.

3. The Harry Potter books are well written. Some critics have likened Rowling's books to boys' adventure stories of several generations ago, or television series of the 1950s and 1960s, stories

such as *Captain Marvel* or *Flash Gordon*, where every episode ends with a cliff-hanger from which the hero escapes at the beginning of the next. This view, I believe, does not do justice to Rowling or her work. One test of a good writer is whether one can read the books over and over with growing pleasure and understanding each time. I read the final book six times over the first six months after its publication and enjoyed it more each time.

Another test is whether one can read a book aloud and find that it communicates well. With a poorly written book you will find yourself wanting to change words and expressions, stumbling over sentences, losing the attention of your hearers. I find the Potter books easy to read aloud, and such reading is pleasurable for hearers. Many parents will testify that they have spent hours reading the books to a rapt audience of their children, their children's friends, and any adults who happen to be present.

A third test is whether these books encourage people to read. As noted above, millions of children have started serious reading for the first time in their lives and have moved on to enjoy other books after first reading the Harry Potter stories.

Fourth, are the books well constructed so that each reading reveals more and more of the interconnectedness of every part of the story? The whole series indeed has this interconnectedness, and Rowling herself says that she knew where her final book would go when her first one was published.

4. There are a multitude of interesting characters in the books. Consider the Weasley family, for example—I would very much like to visit their home for a few days, for each member of the family is a unique and interesting individual who comes to life. Rowling has brought into being an entire portrait gallery of people, both adults and children. One of the most engaging aspects to me, and I think to many readers, is the way these children—especially the main characters, Harry, Hermione, and Ron—grow up book-by-book and eventually become young adults with a depth of maturity that is admirable. Their speech and actions reveal their increasing depth of character. In contrast to Rowling's revelation of their character, poor writing tells readers what to think rather than engaging them

and getting them to think, to reflect, and to draw their own conclusions about who is admirable and why.

5. This noticeable maturing of the children into admirably moral adults leads to another very significant reason for my respect for the seven Harry Potter books. These stories are imbued with a strong message about moral behavior. What are some examples of this? There are beautiful and enjoyable human relationships among the characters, and there is a depth of commitment and faithfulness among them.

The characteristics celebrated in the relationships are friendship, loyalty, integrity, kindness, and mutual service. In each one of the books we see Harry Potter prepared to set aside his own success in order to serve his friends. These are qualities that every reader can and should honor and embrace, for these qualities are honored in every page of these books, not intermittently or in a shallow manner, but as the fundamental moral backdrop of the story.

6. Further, I should add that there is a very clear portrayal of the distinction between good and evil. No reader, of whatever age, can be in doubt about which characters are good and which are bad, which are admirable and which are loathsome. I recall reading an article by a doctor who worked with deeply troubled young people who were growing up in appalling circumstances, their parents often involved in all kinds of crime and unsavory behavior. This doctor said that even the most damaged children only identified with the good characters in the Harry Potter stories. None of the children wished to be Voldemort or Malfoy, for example.

Indeed, Rowling has made her bad characters so unlikable that some critics have charged her with being too simplistic about good and evil. However, this is a foolish charge for the books offer many instances in which the main characters have to learn and mature in moral wisdom—often through their mistakes. One very moving example comes in the last book where Ron has to return to Harry and Hermione and apologize very profoundly for deserting them when the going was tough and when their search for the Horcruxes, which would help them destroy Voldemort, proves to be long, wearisome, and unproductive. The presentation of this struggle to achieve moral wisdom and growth is, I believe, one of the greatest strengths of the Potter books.

Another fascinating example of moral complexity comes with two of the bad characters in the series. The parents of Draco Malfoy are servants of the Dark Lord. However, they are not wholly given up to evil; rather, there are still traces of genuine humanness in them, expressed in their love for their son. Because of this love Draco's mother helps Harry escape from Voldemort by pretending that he is dead. Like Rahab or the Hebrew midwives, Draco's mother lies to protect someone from death. "Love covers a multitude of sins" in her case. Someone who loves is not utterly lost and can still be reached by truth.

Further on this subject of good and evil, the books set out both evil's appalling destructiveness to human life and the beneficial fruit of treating people with justice, kindness, mercy, faithfulness, integrity, and love. It is particularly significant that the books recognize that goodness and faithfulness in relationships come at a price in terms of service, self-giving, and the loss of self-centeredness. Virtue is rewarded primarily in terms of character development and the increasing depths of relationships among the characters, rather than through the attainment of popularity or success.

7. Finally, I see the Potter books as valuable because they consistently include the three fundamental themes—echoes of Eden—that can be found as a subtext in almost all good literature: the beauty of creation, the appalling reality of evil, and the universal human longing for redemption and a better world. These themes touch the way the world truly is, the way God has made the world, and the way he has made us and called us to live within his world.

As a Christian, I am fascinated by the fact that the stories show how a better life comes primarily through self-sacrifice. Any careful rereading of each of the books will reveal that this is a constant theme all through the series. It is brought out unmistakably in the fourth book, *Harry Potter and the Goblet of Fire*. In this book Harry is prepared to sacrifice himself on behalf of his friends, whom he loves and to whom he has a deep loyalty.

At the heart of all of the books in the series is a reference back to Harry's mother, who died when he was a baby in order to save his life from evil in the person of Lord Voldemort. Rowling says that the mother's death on Harry's behalf is an example of the most powerful act imaginable, the strongest force in the universe, self-sacrificing love.

I will return shortly to the theme of self-sacrifice as expressed in the final book of the series, but before I do, we need to reflect further on the criticisms made by Christians. Because this theme of self-sacrifice runs all through the series, it is extraordinary to me that there has been such a violent and negative response by Christians. This negative response is tragic for many reasons.

Responses to the Criticisms from Christians

1. The Word of God certainly calls Christians to be discerning, to take every thought captive and make it obedient to Christ, and to destroy obstacles set up against the knowledge of God (see, for example, Rom. 12:1–2; 2 Cor. 10:4–5; 1 Thess. 5:19). But at the same time, the Word of God calls us to be prepared to celebrate anything that is good and true wherever it is found. For example, Paul says in Philippians 4:8, "Finally, brothers, whatever is true, whatever is honorable, whatever is just, whatever is pure, whatever is lovely, whatever is commendable, if there is any excellence, if there is anything worthy of praise, think about these things." The emphasis on self-sacrifice as the central virtue of human life in the Harry Potter books is something that should be celebrated by Christians. We live in a culture where self-centeredness is a constant theme of much popular entertainment, and to find books that children love and that are emphasizing precisely the opposite should be a cause of great rejoicing.

2. We saw earlier that one cause of distress about the Harry Potter books is their critics' deep suspicion of fantasy. Christians who voice this criticism insist that fantasy and magic are very closely bound together, and that all magic is prohibited to the Christian as necessarily leading to the occult. I have pointed out that the same

criticism is made of the Narnia stories and *The Hobbit* and *The Lord of the Rings*. How should we respond to the criticism of fantasy?

First, we should remind ourselves, again, that all children indulge in fantasy play from a very early age. A child, without any prompting from adults, will take the family dog, cat, hamster, rabbit, or any other pet animal or bird and will pretend that this creature is a thinking, feeling, talking, and reacting person. Often a child will dress an animal in clothes as a part of this game. In the child's mind a fantasy is taking shape, magic is happening, a world of his or her own imaginative making is springing into being.

Any small child will do the same thing with toys: a teddy bear, or a doll, or a soft squirrel, a lamb, or any other creature. I suppose every parent has seen his or her child having a tea party in which toys are dressed, made to sit at a table, and given real or imaginary food and drink on little plates and cups. The child tells all her guests sitting at the table precisely what to do and when to do it as if they were actual persons. I was taking my little four-year-old granddaughter to nursery school one day, and we had to drive along a very bumpy section of road. She suddenly said to her doll: "Dolly, behave yourself! Sit still! This is not a trampoline!"

Every adult who has ever spent time with children will have seen and heard such behavior repeatedly. Sometimes these fantasy games that children play will last for weeks or months and will have an extraordinary inner consistency. Sometimes there will be a "magic word" that has to be spoken, or a "spell" that the child will say or perform before the game can begin or the fantasy world can be reentered.

At a slightly older age children will do the same thing with "action figures" of various kinds. And in this kind of game a child may either invent his own world or use a world from a favorite movie, television show, or story. None of this should trouble a parent in any way. To create another world like this is a foundational part of being a human made in the image of God, the God who called worlds into being and who made us as little likenesses of himself. In addition, we see children exercising dominion over these worlds that they have made, and this also is fundamental to what it means to be the image of God and is a needed element of a child's interacting with the world. An active imagination that can create, enter into, and rule over fantasy worlds seems to be an essential part of childhood and development. Parents need to do everything they can to encourage and commend this kind of play rather than discourage and crush it as dangerous.

It is because this element of fantasy is so foundational to our humanity that Beatrix Potter's books are the best-selling children's stories ever written. Again, anyone who knows little children at all recognizes that when they are playing in their imaginary world, they know perfectly well that it is an imaginary world. Children have no difficulty differentiating between the world of their imagination and the real world.

Second, I will respond to the criticism of fantasy by quoting C. S. Lewis at some length. In this passage he is answering the charge that fantasy is "unrealistic" and too far removed from our ordinary human life, and that, therefore, an author would serve readers better by writing realistic stories rather than fantastic ones. Concerning fantasy in *The Lord of the Rings*, Lewis says:

> "But why," (some ask) "why, if you have a serious comment to make on the real life of men, must you do it by talking about a phantasmagoric never-never land of your own?" Because, I take it, one of the main things the author wants to say is that the real life of men is of that mythical and heroic quality. One can see the principle at work in his characterization. Much that in a realistic work would be done by "character delineation" is here done simply by making the character an elf, a dwarf, or a hobbit [or, we may note, a wizard]. The imagined beings have their insides on the outside; they are visible souls. And Man as a whole, Man pitted against the universe, have we seen him at all till we see that he is like a hero in a fairy tale? In the book (*The Lord of the Rings*) Eomer rashly contrasts "the green earth" with "legends." Aragorn replies that the green earth itself is "a mighty matter of legend."
>
> The value of the myth is that it takes all the things we know and restores to them the rich significance which has been hidden

by "the veil of familiarity." The child enjoys his cold meat (otherwise dull to him) by pretending it is buffalo, just killed with his own bow and arrow. And the child is wise. The real meat comes back to him more savoury for having been dipped in a story; you might say that only then is it the real meat. If you are tired of the real landscape, look at it in a mirror. By putting bread, gold, horse, apple, or the very roads into a myth, we do not retreat from reality: we rediscover it. As long as the story lingers in our mind, the real things are more themselves. This book applies the treatment not only to bread or apple but to good and evil, to our endless perils, our anguish, and our joys. By dipping them in myth we see them more clearly.[1]

Lewis is right; by "dipping" good and evil in myth, in fantasy, in an alternative universe, we see them more clearly than we tend to see them in "real life." The people in a fantasy world are indeed "visible souls." Adults sometimes lose the capacity they had as children to live in worlds of their imagination, and this is not a gain but a sorry loss. Yet, a good story, a fine fantasy, can restore this capacity to the most jaded adult and help to make his or her own daily life more interesting—and more serious. In her wizards and witches, Rowling has simply given us "visible souls" in whom good and evil are readily apparent.

3. We return here to the charge that Harry Potter books are evil because they contain magic, witches, wizards, spells, and the like. As we have seen, the same criticisms have been made of Lewis's and Tolkien's books, even though both of these authors are known by the critics to have been committed Christians. Because magic is a part of the Potter books, the Narnia books, and *The Lord of the Rings*, some claim that these books may have the effect of interesting children in the occult.

What has been said above in the response to the criticism of fantasy applies here also, because we are actually dealing with the same issue. None of these books encourages occult practice. The magic is simply a part of the imaginative worlds that Lewis,

---

[1]C. S. Lewis, "A Review of J. R. R. Tolkien's *Lord of the Rings*," in *Essay Collection and Other Short Pieces*, ed. Lesley Walmsley (London: HarperCollins, 1991), 524–25.

Tolkien, and Rowling have created. In such an imaginary world, people can become invisible, animals talk, mythical creatures like unicorns and centaurs exist, and rings and spells work wonders. In all of these books the magic serves to help us see the battle between good and evil more clearly. Magic is simply a device to unveil the world of virtue and vice to us.

Some Christians have gone on record as stating that they believe that Rowling is purposely and explicitly teaching occult and even satanic practice. Whole books have been written seeking to show the great detail of her allegedly wicked plan to subvert children into fascination with the forbidden world of sorcery and the demonic. However, Rowling herself has repeatedly stated that she has no interest in the occult or magic and that she certainly does not wish to promote it; indeed, she was astonished when she first heard that people had made this criticism.

As a fellow Christian, I have to say I am profoundly ashamed of some of the attacks made on Rowling by Christians, for some of them are no better than malicious gossip, and malicious gossip is itself a disciplinable sin according to Scripture.

This brings us to a very basic point: how are we to react to our culture?

Responding to Culture as Christians

Some 450 years ago John Calvin encouraged people to read books by the great writers from Greece and Rome. He wrote instructions for the teachers in the school system he designed in Geneva, Switzerland, asking that they have the students read the great classics of Greece and Rome that were pagan and non-Christian. And his instructions require that the teachers not criticize them, but rather encourage the students to celebrate what is good in them and learn from the truth that they could find in them. Calvin said on another occasion that it is a blasphemy against the Holy Spirit to deny that pagan writers like Plato wrote many things that are true and helpful.

Therefore, in reading profane authors, the admirable light of truth displayed in them should remind us, that the human mind, however much fallen and perverted from its original integrity, is still adorned and invested with admirable gifts from its Creator. If we reflect that the Spirit of God is the only fountain of truth, we will be careful, as we would avoid offering insult to him, not to reject or condemn truth wherever it appears. In despising the gifts, we insult the Giver [Battles has here: "by holding the gifts of the Spirit in slight esteem, we contemn and reproach the Spirit himself." "Contemn" means to scorn, deride, dishonor, blaspheme. The French and Latin of Calvin's original both have a very strong expression here; so "insult the Giver" is not sufficiently powerful.] How, then, can we deny that truth must have beamed on those ancient lawgivers who arranged civil order and discipline with so much equity? Shall we say that the philosophers, in their exquisite researches and skillful description of nature, were blind? Shall we deny the possession of intellect to those who drew up rules for discourse, and taught us to speak in accordance with reason? Shall we say that those who, by the cultivation of the medical art, expended their industry in our behalf were only raving? What shall we say of the mathematical sciences? Shall we deem them to be the dreams of madmen? No, we cannot read the writings of the ancients on these subjects without the highest admiration; an admiration which their excellence will not allow us to withhold. But shall we deem anything to be noble and praiseworthy, without tracing it to the hand of God? Far from us be such ingratitude; an ingratitude not chargeable even on heathen poets, who acknowledged that philosophy and laws, and all useful arts, were the inventions of the gods.[2]

We must be prepared to follow Calvin's counsel in our day when it comes to the Harry Potter series or any other product of our culture.

We are called by God's Word to do good to all people, and especially to those who are of the household of faith. Rowling claims to be a Christian believer in God and she worships at either an Anglican church or a Church of Scotland congregation near her

---

[2]John Calvin, *Institutes of the Christian Religion*, trans. Henry Beveridge, rev. ed. (Peabody, MA: Hendrickson, 2008), 2.2.25.

home. Attacks on her, whether from ignorance of her convictions or from a failure to read her books or from a refusal to give her books a charitable reading—all such attacks are disobedient to the Scriptures. For those of you who have made the effort to read Rowling's books with care and yet are still troubled by heroes and villains in the form of wizards, let me urge you to think prayerfully about my responses here. In the end you may disagree with me, but I plead with you to think and speak with grace and gentleness about Rowling and her books, and also about the work of Lewis and Tolkien if you are still troubled about their use of magic.

Harry Potter and the Deathly Hallows

Coming back to the theme of self-sacrifice in the Harry Potter books, we turn our attention to the final book in the series, *Harry Potter and the Deathly Hallows*. What is this book about? At its heart Rowling's last Potter book is a reflection on the two biblical quotations included in the story: "Where your treasure is, there will your heart be also," and "The last enemy that shall be destroyed is death."

But what about the story—where does the action take the reader? As background to my defense of Rowling's series, I will summarize some of the main features of the plot. This may be challenging for those who have not read the books, but please bear with me. Only as we understand certain details of the plot will we see how central is the theme of self-sacrifice to all that Rowling has written in her Potter series.

As we read the final book, we discover that the story line hinges on the quest for the "Deathly Hallows." These are three objects of great power that were produced long ago by the creative wisdom of wizards. One of these is the Invisibility Cloak, which has been passed down in Harry's family, a cloak that will make the wearer completely invisible. The possibilities of abusing the cloak to gain power over others are obvious. The second is the Resurrection Stone, which gives the holder a limited power over death. Again, the temptations inherent in such power are evident. The third is the Elder Wand, a wand that is invincible in battle. This wand has led to the violent death of many of those who owned it, because others have lusted after its power.

A very important part of the story is Harry's discovery that his hero, Albus Dumbledore, for many years the headmaster of Hogwarts, the wizard school, was far from perfect at an earlier stage of his life. When he was just seventeen or eighteen, Dumbledore gave himself up to the quest of two of these objects. He was uninterested in the cloak, for he knew spells that could make him invisible; but he wanted the Elder Wand so that he could wield power on behalf of the wizard community. He also wanted the Resurrection Stone so that he might hold power over death.

Dumbledore was joined in this quest by a young wizard from the Continent, Gellert Grindelwald. The two of them became carried away by their search for these objects, and Albus allowed his heart to be captivated by the lust for power at this time in his life. It is Harry's discovering of this aspect of Dumbledore's early life that leads to much of the tension in the book, for Harry realizes that the man to whom he has looked as a mentor and father figure, a fountain of wisdom and goodness, was deeply flawed as a young man. Albus's lust for power and the dreams of conquest that filled his mind for a brief time led to the childhood death of his deeply troubled sister, Ariana, and to a sadly strained relationship with his younger brother, Aberforth.

Harry has to come to terms with the loss of his view of Dumbledore as perfect. More importantly, Harry also has to wrestle in turn with the quest for the Deathly Hallows. The question at the heart of the book is this: Will Harry keep going with the task that Dumbledore has given him, the task of finding and destroying the Horcruxes created by Lord Voldemort, Horcruxes that contain pieces of his fractured and wicked soul? The central issue is, where will Harry's treasure lie? For where his treasure is, there will be the devotion of his heart. Will his treasure be the longing for power? Or will his treasure be the commitment to fight against evil, whatever the cost to himself?

What are the Horcruxes? Voldemort has created the six Horcruxes: the ring with the Resurrection Stone, the Diary of Tom

Riddle (his own birth name), the locket of Regulus Black, the Huffle-puff house cup, the Ravenclaw diadem, the snake Nagini—all these to keep himself invulnerable. This is his plan: if his soul is divided, and the separated parts hidden away, then no one will ever be able to defeat him.

Voldemort's treasure is a lust for power, power over others at any cost, power and dominion without any moral consideration. He is a liar, a deceiver, a betrayer, and a murderer—clearly modeled on Satan in the Scriptures. Everything he does has the purpose of increasing his power over others. Voldemort also has a fear of death; and, so, to try to cheat death, he creates the Horcruxes. One beautiful irony is that unbeknownst to him, he in fact created a seventh Horcrux when he tried to kill the infant Harry. Harry himself is that seventh Horcrux, and so Voldemort's soul is even more fractured and vulnerable than he realizes, vulnerable especially when he is faced with Harry.

Will Harry pursue this task of searching out and destroying the Horcruxes, as this is necessary for Voldemort to be defeated? Or will Harry become distracted by the Deathly Hallows and give himself to searching for these instead? Like the young Dumbledore he can find reasons why this would seem a wise and noble thing to do. But where is Harry's treasure? Will it be Hallows or Horcruxes? What will control the decisions of his heart: power and holding death at bay, or the task of saving others in the commitment to destroy Voldemort, even if it should prove to cost him his life?

After struggling with this decision, with even Ron pushing him toward the Hallows—for Ron assumes that the Elder Wand will enable Harry to destroy Voldemort, the evil lord—Harry chooses the path of giving himself to destroy the Horcruxes. As he pursues this path, his life is endangered repeatedly, for the path of destroying evil is the path of self-sacrifice, of being prepared to die for the sake of others.

Harry's treasure is the love of others, not power for himself, not fame, not long life, not success, not money—nothing but the willingness to serve others and to do so at any cost. Because this is his treasure, his heart is committed to pursuing a path that will protect others from Lord Voldemort, a path that will deliver them from evil, a path that will enable them to live in peace and security.

Ron and Hermione join Harry in this task, and in joining him they choose the same way of being committed to laying down their lives for the well-being of others. Indeed, we may say that every good character in this final book is prepared to make this choice, that is, to be ready to sacrifice his or her life to save others. We see this at the beginning when Harry's friends disguise themselves as Harry to help him escape. They all risk death, all thirteen who come to help him: those six disguised as Harry, and those seven who carry Harry and his look-alikes to safety. One of them, Mad-Eye Moody, does die in this venture. "Greater love has no one than this, that someone lay down his life for his friends" (John 15:13). And Moody dies. Another is wounded in the battle.

The Weasley family puts their safety at risk by taking Harry into their home. Ron and Hermione are in constant danger of injury and death when they join Harry in the search for Horcruxes; and they are perfectly aware of this endangerment of themselves and of those they love. Harry tries to dissuade his friends from joining him, but they are committed at great cost to themselves and their families. Harry's friends Fred and George, Neville, Luna, Lupin, Tonks, Dobby the House Elf—all of them are prepared to give up their lives for those they love, and some of them do. Indeed, this is the truth for more than fifty who die, and of countless others who are prepared to give their lives to fight evil.

It is also the truth of Severus Snape—who at the last is revealed as a man motivated by an undying love for the deceased Lily Potter, the mother of Harry. He too has spent his life on the knife-edge of danger, braving constantly the wrath of the evil lord while serving the cause of good. At all times he has been Dumbledore's ally and the enemy of the Dark Lord. Snape, too, dies in the service of others. Harry names one of his sons after him, Albus Severus: *Albus* because of his deep admiration for Dumbledore; *Severus* because Harry has at last come to the realization that, despite all appearances to the contrary, Snape was in fact the bravest man Harry has ever known.

Self-sacrifice is a central theme in all the books. As mentioned above, Harry's mother gave her life for him when he was a baby, and the power of this love—the greatest power in the universe, according to Rowling—has been his protection all his life. Now in the final book we see Harry taking his turn, not just once, but several times, in being prepared to give his life as a ransom for his friends. There are many echoes throughout the book of the temptation narratives in the Gospels, and also of the accounts of Christ preparing for his suffering and death.

Harry has to set his face toward his death, just as Jesus set his face toward Jerusalem. He has to recognize that his free offering of himself to death is what Dumbledore was preparing him for, all through his years of friendship and schooling at Hogwarts. When Harry sees his friends suffering and dying in the fight against Voldemort, he is eager to give himself up, to drink the cup that has been prepared for him. He must leave his dearest friends, Ron and Hermione, behind, lest they try to dissuade him from his chosen path, and he must commit himself to take his final walk alone. When that final walk comes, he is in fact comforted by the appearance of his dead parents, James and Lily, and his dead friends Sirius and Lupin.

Though he gave himself to the pursuit of the Horcruxes and gave himself to death out of love for others, although he gave up the search for the way of power through gaining the Deathly Hallows, in the end Harry does gain the Hallows. The Invisibility Cloak he possessed for many years, for it was an heirloom passed down in his family. He used it wisely—not to gain himself power or wisdom—but to serve the needs of others and to help in his lifelong task of overcoming Voldemort.

The Resurrection Stone comes to him as a gift from Dumbledore, and again, he uses it wisely, not to try to defeat death for himself or to gain power, but as a blessed comfort in calling his parents and friends to him in his hour of need. Then he discards it and makes no attempt to find it again. He knows that there will be a final victory over death, a victory that cannot be gained by magic, a victory that will be permanent and filled with joy when death itself, the last enemy, shall be destroyed.

The Elder Wand he wins in battle without deceit and without killing its former masters. Then he immediately gives it up after using it merely to repair his own wand. He has no wish to have an undefeatable wand, a wand that has been abused and killed for by the power-hungry throughout its history.

Harry wins his battles not by wisdom and not by strength, but by things thought foolish and powerless by the world. He wins by commitment to the truth, by loyalty to his friends, and by serving them—including those who are despised in the "world's" eyes, people like the goblin whose life he saves and the house elves whose dignity he restores.

Above all, he wins his battles by self-sacrificing love. At the climax of the book he walks calmly to his death, and his enemies laugh at his folly. He does not draw his wand; he does not fight; he simply gives himself up and Voldemort curses him with the curse of death. Precisely because he offers himself up to death and to defeat—just as does Christ—he conquers death, for it cannot hold him.

Remarkably, just as with Satan at the cross, Voldemort himself is struck down by his own act of seeking to destroy Harry. He survives this encounter for a brief time, but with his power greatly reduced. He can no longer destroy at will; his power has waned as a result of his own cruelty and of his wicked attempts to destroy Harry.

Harry is restored to life and engages Voldemort for one last time in battle. He has seen what Voldemort will become at death, and he pities him and holds out to him one last hope of repentance: "Try for some remorse," Harry says. But Voldemort will not listen. He attempts for one final time to destroy Harry with the curse of death. However, even in this final confrontation, Harry does not try to kill Voldemort. In battle he seeks to disarm his enemies, rather than to destroy them. Voldemort uses the Elder Wand for one last time, cursing Harry with the terrible death curse, but his curse on Harry rebounds on himself. He destroys himself by his attempt to destroy Harry; just as the Devil defeats himself by seeking to overcome Christ when he puts him on the cross.

It should be evident to anyone reading the above summary how many remarkable parallels to the gospel story there are in this final book of the Harry Potter series. I found myself weeping with joy many, many times as I read and reread this wonderful reflection on the work of Christ.

In the earlier novels it was evident to any careful reader that commitment to the truth, loyalty, service, care for the weak and oppressed, and, above all, self-sacrificing love were the highest values of these stories; and these are of course the highest moral values for a Christian. This is why it was so distressing to see the hysterical criticism poured out on the series by believers, the attempts to ban the books, and the denunciation of Rowling as someone encouraging witchcraft, as someone engaged in the occult, even as someone who is purposefully serving the cause of the Devil.

The themes of truthfulness, loyalty, service, care for the weak and oppressed, and self-sacrificing love, present in the first book, became stronger and stronger as the series progressed. In addition, the theme of the destructiveness of using wisdom and power only for oneself, the theme of how readily power can be abused by those who seek it, and the theme of the abuse of the weak and oppressed by the powerful—these also became stronger and stronger as the successive novels were published and their stories unfolded.

From the very beginning, when the first book was published, Rowling denied that she had any interest in the occult; she denied that she was encouraging witchcraft. I heard her first radio interview in the United States, in which she spoke of the influence of Lewis and Tolkien on her as a writer. Those who are troubled by the magic in these books need to try to see that, just as in the Narnia stories and in *The Lord of the Rings*, it is merely a device to help the author showcase the nature of good and evil, the temptations of self-love, wisdom, and power, and the supreme values at the heart of the gospel of Christ.

More recently J. K. Rowling has acknowledged that she is a Christian believer. As mentioned earlier, she worships at either an

Anglican church or a Church of Scotland congregation, depending on her place of residence. And, as I have been at some pains to show, in the last book Rowling comes right out into the open with her deep understanding of the central themes of the gospel. These Christian themes have at their center the redemptive power of self-sacrificing love.

In addition, almost as an aside, we notice that this last book is the first in which Rowling includes biblical quotations. Inscribed on the tomb of Albus Dumbledore's mother and sister are the words, "Where your treasure is, there will your heart be also."[3] And on the tomb of Harry's parents, James and Lily Potter is this: "The last enemy that shall be destroyed is death."[4] Christians should thank God for J. K. Rowling and for her clear presentation of the central values that are at the core of Christian faith and practice.

---

[3] J. K. Rowling, *Harry Potter and the Deathly Hallows* (New York: Arthur A. Levine, 2007), 325.
[4] Ibid., 328.

9

Shakespeare and a Christian Worldview

Judged by the perennial popularity of his plays, William Shakespeare is the greatest dramatist and one of the finest poets to have written in any language. One mark of this greatness is the way characters come alive and make believable speeches representing extraordinarily diverse views about life in this world. This variety of ways of seeing the human situation can make it difficult to discern Shakespeare's own understanding of the human condition. However, I believe that at a deeper level than the notions of particular characters in his plays, we will find an underlying worldview that is thoroughly Christian.

Shakespeare lived from 1564 to 1616. Yet, when people were surveyed in the year 2000, he ranked far ahead of anyone else as the person of the last millennium, and these were surveys that included thinkers such as Marx, who had a very profound impact on vast sections of the world; other political leaders, like Roosevelt or Churchill, Hitler or Stalin; and religious figures like Luther, Mother Teresa, or particular popes. But no one came even close to Shakespeare, in terms of either his popularity or his impact upon the world; he stood head and shoulders above everyone else. What accounts for this enduring and profound impact on people, not only in the English-speaking world but also around the globe?

Many of us will have seen his plays (in English or in translation) on the stage. I will never forget my own stage introduction to Shakespeare. When I was twelve our English teacher arranged for our class to go and see *Romeo and Juliet* at the Old Vic Theatre in

London. Dame Judi Dench, a young actress at that time just beginning her career, was playing Juliet. I was entranced by her, by the play, by the theater, by Shakespeare—and I have been ever since. Where we live in St. Louis there are free performances of Shakespeare's plays in Forest Park each summer. They are well done and very popular. One of our sons lives in St. Louis, and he and our daughter-in-law began to take their two sons, our grandsons, when they were little. I remember the boys, one four years old and the other two, staying awake till almost 11:00 p.m., watching *The Tempest*—not the easiest play, one would have thought, for small children, but they enjoyed it thoroughly.

Of course, not all theater experiences are so pleasurable. My wife and I took my mother to see a production of *A Midsummer Night's Dream* at the Royal Shakespeare Theatre in Stratford-on-Avon. It was to be a special treat for her as she had not been able to go for many years. I telephoned at the time I was booking the tickets and asked whether the play was suitable for children (not because any of us were children, but because I am aware how directors can take appalling license with their productions of a play). I was assured that it was fine and was told that that particular afternoon there would be several parties of school children attending. With eager anticipation, for my mother especially, we drove up to Stratford full of excitement. However, the production was anything but fine!

Shakespeare's magical play set in the enchanted woods had been turned into something very different. The first sign of trouble (and of the problems with the director's vision of the play) was that the people of Athens were dressed as puritans (I assume that was the intention) in stark black and white. They stood rigidly still around the circumference of the stage and spoke their lines in monotones. I thought that maybe, like Rousseau, this director believed that civilization inhibits personal freedom: "Man is born free, but is everywhere in chains." In contrast to the rigid constraint of life in Athens, the forest was a scene of complete lack of inhibitions. The fairies behaved as if they were nymphomaniacs, as if they were crazed for sex, and entirely without inhibition in their dress or actions. The encounter between Bottom and Titania was turned into a scene of horribly explicit bestiality.

By this time several of the school groups had already got up and left the theater. My mother, who is not prudish or puritanical, was shocked to the core. The three of us were speechless. This is the worst example I have ever seen of a stage or film director completely ignoring the intentions of the artist.

Thankfully this kind of outrageous foolishness is rare, so I would encourage readers not to assume that such violence to the intent of the author is regularly done in productions of Shakespeare's plays. Sometimes one may have questions about the director's interpretation of particular characters or aspects of a play, but the problems are very rarely this severe.

I am sure that most readers of this will have seen some of the recent film versions of Shakespeare's plays, for many of these have been extraordinarily well done and have become very popular. Some of the best have been Kenneth Branagh's productions of *Henry V, Much Ado about Nothing,* and *Hamlet.* Also there are outstanding versions of *Twelfth Night* with Imogen Stubbs as Viola, *The Merchant of Venice* with Al Pacino as Shylock, *Romeo and Juliet* with Leonardo DiCaprio as Romeo, and *Othello* with Kenneth Branagh as Iago and Lawrence Fishburne as Othello. These are just a few of the excellent films of Shakespeare's plays made over the past twenty years. There is also a complete cycle of the plays done for BBC television in the 1970s and 1980s, and almost all of these were very fine. I remember, in particular, *As You Like It* with Helen Mirren playing the part of Rosalind.

I mention these as an encouragement to readers to develop their own lists of favorite productions, and also to persevere if their introduction to Shakespeare on stage is similar to our appalling experience of expecting to watch *A Midsummer Night's Dream* and having to view another play entirely.

What about William Shakespeare the man? There is not much that can be said with confidence, for Shakespeare was a very private man about whose personal life we know very little. What can we say? We know a bit about the family he was born into in Stratford, a line of information about his childhood and education, maybe three or four lines about his marriage and family, a paragraph about his personal life in London while he worked in the theater, and another very brief paragraph about his few years in Stratford after his retirement, when he worked on final manuscript versions of his plays.

This paucity of information has given rise to endless speculation, some of it book-length or series-length on television. Some of the recreations of his life are fascinating, but almost all of them are entirely speculative. So little is known about him that several scholars have tried to make their reputations, and their fortunes, by proposing that someone else must have written the plays, someone more formally educated, someone better known. The suggestions range from royalty, to nobility, to other famous dramatists, to men of letters—even to a syndicate of writers. This, however, is all nonsense.

We can speak with more confidence about Shakespeare's career in the theater. He was an actor, a member of a troupe of actors numbering about seven or eight men and a couple of boys (for the women's parts). This meant that Shakespeare would regularly take part in the plays that were being performed (he played the ghost in Hamlet, for example) while also writing new plays. He was a part-owner of a theater company, together with his fellow actors. This company built its own theater. It also put on plays each season before the royal court; for example, *Twelfth Night* was shown during the period after Christmas. The royal season lasted about two weeks, beginning on December 26, and four or five plays were performed during that time; there was another brief royal season at Lent with two or three plays performed.

The main work of the company was the two London seasons held each year, one in spring and the other in autumn. The company's practice was to present a different production each weekday afternoon and then to introduce a new play into their repertory every two weeks. This meant a vast amount of hard work for the actors, who were constantly learning new parts and playing several different roles at the same time. Shakespeare himself was always writing new plays at the same time as helping with the current productions. These plays and their stage presentations had to be of good quality, for at that time about one third of the population in London attended the theaters. This was perhaps the best theater-educated audience that any group of actors has ever had to play before. They also had to be quality plays and presentations as there were several other competing companies offering their productions to this very discerning population. In addition to these seasons in London and at the royal court, the company traveled around the country during the summer, putting on their plays in rural cities.

Glorious Poetry

Shakespeare was a poet, one of the greatest to write verse in English, or in any language. I will include just two examples of his glorious poetry. The first is from *Antony and Cleopatra*. This is taken from a scene where Antony's general Enobarbus is telling Agrippa why Antony will never desert Cleopatra, even though Antony has just agreed to marry Octavia, the sister of Octavius Caesar, in order to seal a peace agreement between the two. Enobarbus describes the first meeting of Antony and Cleopatra on the river Cydnus in Egypt. Read this aloud to help the words come to life. Notice the visual images and the sensuality of his account:

> *Enobarbus*
> I will tell you.
> The barge she sat in, like a burnish'd throne,
> Burn'd on the water; the poop was beaten gold,
> Purple the sails, and so perfumed, that
> The winds were love-sick with them, the oars were silver,
> Which to the tune of flutes kept stroke, and made
> The water which they beat to follow faster,
> As amorous of their strokes. For her own person,
> It beggar'd all description; she did lie
> In her pavilion,—cloth-of-gold of tissue,—
> O'er-picturing that Venus where we see
> The fancy outwork nature; on each side her
> Stood pretty-dimpled boys, like smiling Cupids,

With divers-colour'd fans, whose wind did seem
To glow the delicate cheeks which they did cool,
And what they undid did.

Agrippa
O! rare for Antony.

Enobarbus
Her gentlewomen, like the Nereides,
So many mermaids, tended her i' the eyes,
And made their bends adornings; at the helm
A seeming mermaid steers; the silken tackle
Swell with the touches of those flower-soft hands,
That yarely frame the office. From the barge
A strange invisible perfume hits the sense
Of the adjacent wharfs. The city cast
Her people out upon her, and Antony,
Enthron'd i' the market-place, did sit alone,
Whistling to the air; which, but for vacancy,
Had gone to gaze on Cleopatra too
And made a gap in nature.
        (*Antony and Cleopatra*, act 2, scene 2)

Here is a much briefer example from *Macbeth*, a series of wonderful images about sleep that are justly famous:

Methought I heard a voice cry "Sleep no more!
Macbeth does murder sleep"—the innocent sleep,
Sleep that knits up the raveled sleave of care,
The death of each day's life, sore labor's bath,
Balm of hurt minds, great nature's course,
Chief nourisher in life's feast.
        (*Macbeth*, act 2, scene 2)

These are just two illustrations of Shakespeare's extraordinary gifts as a poet.

The Greatest Playwright

In addition to his remarkable poetic gifts, Shakespeare was, of course, a playwright, and probably the greatest playwright to have written in any language. Altogether, in a fairly brief career he wrote about three dozen plays. Most of these are performed regularly today, four hundred years after they were written. It is probably no exaggeration to say that Shakespearean plays are seen in many places in the world every day of our lives. They have been translated into dozens of languages, and while some of the power of the poetry is lost in translation, the drama is so good that it transcends language and appeals to people in widely divergent cultural settings. The reason for this is that Shakespeare's plays capture the perennial joys and sorrows, weaknesses and strengths, achievements and struggles, successes and failures of our common human condition.

What Shakespeare did in the theater was new. There were fine plays written for the English stage before him—for example, from the young Christopher Marlowe (*Dr. Faustus, Tamburlaine the Great, Edward II, The Jew of Malta*)—but the theater takes on a new and far more significant life as a result of Shakespeare's work.

He took material from a great diversity of sources. Some of his plays have characters and subject matter derived from the world of ancient Greece and Rome—though when dealing with this "classical" material he did not simply write history plays about the past, but tied the themes of each play into his times and the struggles taking place in Britain right then. *Julius Caesar*, written in 1599, is an example of this. It is a "chronicle of the times," to use Shakespeare's own expression. (See James Shapiro's wonderful book *A Year in the Life of William Shakespeare: 1599*, which shows how the plays he wrote in that year—*Hamlet, Julius Caesar, Henry V*, etc.—all reflect in depth upon the current situation.)[1]

In addition, there are plays written on stories from many parts of Europe and from the history and legends of Britain, including many on the lives and times of English kings.

---

[1] James Shapiro, *A Year in the Life of William Shakespeare: 1599* (London: HarperCollins, 2005).

Because Shakespeare is such a great writer, every speech from whatever perspective is powerful and persuasive. We could say that he is the writer with a thousand faces, each of them seemingly authentic and convincing. Many people, including some critics, appear to think that someone can only write about what he or she has personally experienced. But a few moment's reflection will help us to see the folly in such a view, for one would have to imagine Shakespeare being, in private life, both one of the greatest villains the world has ever seen and one of the finest of men: a man who was faithful and unfaithful in marriage and family life; a man who was both kind and cruel; a man of great goodness and of deep evil—all these variations present in his life in constantly shifting patterns.

Elizabeth Jenkins has written with power and humor about this creative genius of Shakespeare and his remarkable ability to get inside very diverse people with insight and understanding:

> The creative mind of the first order is infinitely difficult to understand; Dryden understood it when he said of Shakespeare: "After God, he has created most" . . . . the only thing that deters [countless people] from believing that Shakespeare smothered his wife in a fit of jealousy, was deeply distressed by a second marriage of his mother's, murdered a distinguished guest in the hope of succeeding him in his office, and was finally turned out of doors by his ungrateful children, is that the stories of Othello, Hamlet, Macbeth and Lear were published and widely known before he undertook them.
>
> The highest type of creative genius owes to daily life at once everything and nothing; its implements, its medium, are supplied by observation of the topical existence, but its inspiration lies in the fact that owing to some extraordinary *lusus naturae* (freak of nature) it is in touch with something that encompasses us but that the rest of us do not see; racial memory or basic consciousness, one knows not how to name this vantage ground, and dark as it is to us, there is no doubt that it was equally so to the conscious mind of its possessors. But when they postulated to themselves a human being in a particular situation, something nameless

whispered to them all the rest. How could Shakespeare, three hundred years before anyone had investigated the working of the sub-conscious mind, have understood that though Lady Macbeth had urged her husband not to be appalled by blood, which a little water could wash away, yet when her conscious mind was asleep, she was haunted by the nightmare that she would never get the bloodstains off her hands?[2]

Partly because Shakespeare writes with such depth about the inner workings of the human heart and mind, and with such persuasive power about so many different issues, critics have posited that he himself embraced contradictory views and practices on all sorts of matters. One view says he is a royalist; another says he is an antiroyalist; one sees him as a passionate Protestant, another as a secret Catholic; he is said to be faithful in marriage and at the same time promiscuous, heterosexual and yet homosexual, a cynic and yet an optimist. This is simply because each position held by the characters in his plays is presented with such genuine feeling and conviction.

Hamlet is a classic example of this great variety of interpretations. The divergences of viewpoint arise from Shakespeare's deep insight into the struggles and passions of the inner person. If one watches several different productions of the play, one may find Hamlet presented as any of the following: hero, madman, villain, romantic, misogynist, a man in love with his mother, and so on.

Yet, I am persuaded that at a deeper level than the views of particular characters, deeper than the source material from which Shakespeare crafted his masterpieces, a biblical worldview pervades all that he writes. Shakespeare writes as a Christian, with a Christian way of seeing the world, and with a Christian perspective on the human condition. His plays are filled with echoes of Eden: reflections on the glory, on the tragedy, and on the hope for redemption that are the true story of our situation in this world. Deep truth presented with extraordinary clarity, power, and depth

---

[2]Elizabeth Jenkins, *Jane Austen* (London: Sphere, 1972), 64.

of feeling—these are the primary reasons for the perennial popularity of Shakespeare's work.

His audiences are constantly touched at the most fundamental level of who they are as persons made by and for God, persons wandering far from him, and persons in need of deliverance from their broken lives. These deep chords are struck in the heart whether a person is a professing Christian, a passionate atheist, a Hindu, a Muslim, a postmodern cynic, or whatever one's views about life may be. We see our true condition in the plays of Shakespeare, so rich are the echoes of Eden found there.

Macbeth

For most of the remainder of this chapter we will look at one example, *Macbeth*. I believe this play to be an extraordinary reflection on the nature of evil, one of the most accurate accounts ever written on entrapment into making wicked choices, and the consequences of those choices.

First, the play reflects on the relationship between evil choices in this world and the forces of wickedness in the unseen world.

The Interaction of the Supernatural World of Demons and Witchcraft with This World

When we read the script or watch a production, there are various ways the scenes between Macbeth and the witches are understood today. The following are some of the interpretations I have seen:

1. The director does not know what to do with the witches and so he turns them into a kind of comic relief.

2. Supernatural evil is assumed by the director not to be real at all, and so the witches are turned into images of Macbeth's inner turmoil. These scenes become a look into Macbeth's own diseased mind.

3. The witches are seen as the instruments, or expressions, of impersonal forces of fate that will direct Macbeth's life to inevitable tragedy. Macbeth will have no say in his destiny, for all is written out in the stars for him. In this understanding Shakespeare is turned

into one of the great Greek tragedians, like Aeschylus, Sophocles, or Euripides. Think of the play *Oedipus Rex* as an example, which unfolds the inexorable fate foretold of Oedipus, regardless of the attempts by his mother, himself, or anyone else to thwart this pre-determined destiny and create a different future.

4. Supernatural evil is determinative of events in this world, and human beings are weak and powerless playthings in the hands of forces far beyond their ability to resist. For a presentation of this very gloomy perspective, see Roman Polanski's film, in which it is quite clear that the witches are servants of the pervading and controlling power of darkness. Notice, in particular, how at the end of the film, the scene from the start of the play is repeated—this time with different persons who, like Macbeth at the beginning, are about to have their lives turned upside down by the intervention of the witches, and of the demons who give the witches their power, demons who are behind the evil in this world.

5. The play presents a biblical view very different from the four approaches described above. In this biblical way of seeing reality, there is an interaction between evil supernatural powers and human choices in this world. The witches, as Satan's representatives, sow lies and deceit before Macbeth in their attempt to take a human soul captive to the prince of darkness. However, humans are genuinely significant and can both choose to resist supernatural powers of darkness and seek aid from heaven in their calling to follow good rather than evil.

These five are some of the interpretations of *Macbeth* that one can find on the stage or in movies. The question is, which of these options faithfully represents the viewpoint of the play that Shakespeare had in mind? If we read the text itself, it is clear that Shakespeare does not present a Greek fatalist view of these events. Macbeth is not simply fulfilling a destiny outside his control. After he and his friend Banquo meet the witches, Banquo comments on the way the powers of darkness can assume the appearance of truth, goodness, and light (not that the witches appear like angels of light—they do not—but they do speak some words that are true). Banquo, recognizing the problem, resists the temptation:

> But 'tis strange!
> And oftentimes, to win us to our harm,
> The instruments of darkness tell us truths,
> Win us with honest trifles, to betray's
> In deepest consequence.
>> (act 1, scene 3)

Macbeth, however, chooses to believe the witches for his own advantage, pretending that the witches' words are neither good nor evil. He ignores Banquo's warning for, despite denying that their soliciting of him can be evil or good, Macbeth is already beginning to think of appalling deeds he could do to bring about the witches' prophecy that he will be king.

We should notice, too, how he recognizes that the witches have supernatural knowledge. Macbeth is quite aware that he and Banquo have had the veil between this world and the unseen world drawn back momentarily. The witches, he understands, are speaking for some spiritual higher forces.

> This supernatural soliciting
> Cannot be ill; cannot be good. If ill,
> Why hath it given me earnest of success,
> Commencing in a truth? I am thane of Cawdor.
> If good, why do I yield to that suggestion
> Whose horrid image doth unfix my hair
> And make my seated heart knock at my ribs
> Against the use of nature? Present fears
> Are less than horrible imaginings.
> My thought, whose murder yet is but fantastical,
> Shakes so my single state of man that function
> Is smothered in surmise and nothing is
> But what is not.
>> (act 1, scene 3)

Just a short time later, when Lady Macbeth gets the news from her husband of what the witches have prophesied for his future, we see her discussing whether her husband is too good and kind a man to choose to do what will need to be done to remove King Duncan from power. She fully understands that murder is the only way to bring about the future the witches have foretold for Macbeth, and so we see her calling on the spirits of darkness to come and possess her so that she will put aside all thoughts of compassion, righteousness, and justice and instead be able to join in the murder of her own king, kinsman, and guest. Her direct invocation to Satan contains some of the most terrible words in literature:

> Come, you spirits
> That tend on mortal thoughts, unsex me here,
> And fill me, from the crown to the toe, top-full
> Of direst cruelty! Make thick my blood;
> Stop up the access and passage to remorse,
> That no compunctious visitings of nature
> Shake my fell purpose nor keep peace between
> The effect and it! come to my woman's breasts
> And take my milk for gall, you murd'ring ministers,
> Wherever in your sightless substances
> You wait on nature's mischief! Come, thick night,
> And pall thee in the dunnest smoke of hell,
> That my keen knife see not the wound it makes,
> Nor heaven peep through the blanket of the dark
> To cry "Hold, Hold!"
> > (act 1, scene 5)

The Reality of Human Significance

Shakespeare clearly believes that there is the appalling reality of the evil supernatural, an unseen world, a realm of darkness that can impact this world of our senses. At the same time, he makes it clear that there is true significance for the persons whose stories are told in the drama. It is this reality of human volition that turns Macbeth into such a profound tragedy.

If, as in many modern productions, Macbeth is presented as a puppet on the wheel of fate, or as someone with a personality flaw that makes him powerless to resist evil, then the tragedy is not so deep or so shocking. It is the reality of the choices made by Macbeth and Lady Macbeth—choices that they are not compelled to make—that renders the tragedy so sad and touches us so deeply, for we all recognize ourselves in this story of how choice changes the directions of our lives in all-encompassing ways.

Shakespeare's play is a study of descent into evil by both Macbeth and Lady Macbeth as they make real choices that change the course of human history. The play opens with Macbeth as a hero. Shakespeare's purpose here is to enable us as the audience to identify with Macbeth, to see his good qualities, and to admire him so that we will have sorrow in our hearts for him as the good is thrown away. If Macbeth and Lady Macbeth were puppets controlled by a fate over which they had no power, inexorable deterministic forces in history, then there might still be tragedy too, and pity; but it would be a different kind of tragedy than that dramatized by Shakespeare. It would be a Greek or Hindu tragedy, but not a Christian tragedy.

To underline the true human significance of Macbeth and the biblical nature of the story, Macbeth is given—even to the end of the play—some of the most beautiful poetic lines that we find in all of Shakespeare. The loveliness of Macbeth's words, even as he descends ever further into the pit of evil and loses all hope for the future, heighten for us the nature of his ongoing human glory as, in the same moment, we are appalled by the shame of his fall into terrible wickedness.

> Had I but died an hour before this chance,
> I had lived a blessed time; for from this instant
> There's nothing serious in mortality;
> All is but toys; renown and grace is dead;
> The wine of life is drawn, and the mere lees
> Is left this vault to brag of.
> (act 2, scene 3)

The Consequences of Choices Present a Fully Biblical Understanding of Evil

In the biblical account of the fall of Adam and Eve we see the far-reaching consequences of their choice to disobey God. Every aspect of their lives is affected: their relationship with God and God's with them, their relationship to themselves, their relationship with each other, their dominion over themselves and the world, their bodies and eternal souls, and even creation itself.

Alienation is brought into every part of their lives. In *Macbeth* we find Shakespeare following this biblical story as he sets out what happens after the dreadful choice that Macbeth and his wife make when they decide to murder Duncan and so seize the throne for themselves.

1. First, there is loss of fellowship with God. We see Macbeth making the conscious choice to do what he knows will make him an enemy of God, just as Paul writes that we become enemies of God in our minds because of our evil behavior (Col. 1:21). Hear Macbeth's words as he hardens his conscience against God and against the prospect of God's just judgment:

> If it were done when 'tis done, then 'twere well
> It were done quickly. If the assassination
> Could trammel up the consequences, and catch,
> With his surcease, success, that but this blow
> Might be the be-all and the end-all here,
> But here, upon this bank and shoal of time,
> We'd jump the life to come. But in these cases
> We still have judgment here, that we but teach
> bloody instructions, which, being taught, return
> To plague the inventor. This even-handed justice
> Commends the ingredients of our poisoned chalice
> To our own lips.
>   (act 1, scene 7)

2. Making oneself an enemy of God has a second effect: God is made an enemy of the one who turns against him. In reflecting on his own revolt against God and his commandments, Macbeth

adds his recognition that he will indeed face eternal damnation, ultimate separation from God, because of the life of Duncan crying out to God against the crime of shedding his blood:

> . . . his virtues
> Will plead like angels, trumpet-tongued, against
> The deep damnation of his taking-off.
>> (act 1, scene 7)

Once his choice to murder the king is made, we see Macbeth finding it impossible to pray, for he senses that heaven is now closed to him and that God will no longer listen. Here Macbeth echoes the words of Isaiah when the prophet says that our iniquities are so great that God can no longer hear our prayers (Isa. 59:2).

Macbeth
One cried "God bless us!" and "Amen!" the other,
As they had seen me with these hangman's hands,
List'ning their fear. I could not say "Amen!"
When they did say "God bless us!"

Lady Macbeth
Consider it not so deeply.

Macbeth
But wherefore could not I pronounce "Amen"?
I had most need of blessing, and "Amen"
Stuck in my throat.
>> (act 2, scene 2)

3. Third, we see in Macbeth and Lady Macbeth a deep alienation from their inner selves. Guilt and shame haunt them both and give them a sense of uncleanness even in their own eyes:

Lady Macbeth
These deeds must not be thought
After these ways. So, it will make us mad.

Macbeth
Me thought I heard a voice cry "Sleep no more!
Macbeth does murder sleep"—the innocent sleep,
Sleep that knits up the raveled sleave of care,
The death of each day's life, sore labor's bath,
Balm of hurt minds, great nature's second course,
Chief nourisher in life's feast . . .
How is't with me when every noise appalls me?
What hands are here? Ha! they pluck out my eyes!
Will all great Neptune's ocean wash this blood
Clean from my hand? No. This my hand will rather
The multitudinous seas incarnadine,
Making the green one red.
    (act 2, scene 2)

In the following passage we see Macbeth using the biblical language of the snake in the garden to describe the power of evil in their lives from this point onward:

Lady Macbeth
    Things without all remedy
Should be without regard. What's done is done.

Macbeth
We have scorched the snake, not killed it.
She'll close and be herself, whilst our poor malice
Remains in danger of her former tooth.
    (act 3, scene 2)

4. The self-destruction that evil choices engender leads them both to the loss of dominion over their own bodies, sleep, dreams, sanity, even life itself:

But let the frame of things disjoint, both the worlds suffer,
Ere we will eat our meal in fear and sleep
In the affliction of these terrible dreams
That shake us nightly. Better be with the dead,

Than on the torture of the mind to lie
In restless ecstasy.
> (act 3, scene 2)

Macbeth becomes so full of evil that he desires to crush his own
conscience, that he will no longer have to see the wicked works
of his own hands:

O, full of scorpions is my mind . . . !
. . . Come, sealing night,
Scarf up the tender eye of pitiful day,
And with thy bloody and invisible hand
Cancel and tear to pieces that great bond
Which keeps me pale!
> (act 3, scene 2)

Later we see Lady Macbeth losing her sanity and being a danger
to her own life as her guilt begins to consume her. These are the
words of her doctor, who has heard shocking things from Lady
Macbeth as she sleepwalks:

Infected minds
To their deaf pillows will discharge their secrets.
More needs she the divine than the physician.
God, God forgive us all! Look after her;
Remove from her the means of all annoyance,
And still keep eyes upon her.
> (act 5, scene 1)

5. There is a breakdown of relationships between Macbeth and
others, and this spreads like a disease, affecting not only Macbeth
and his wife, but the rest of the Scottish people. Everyone becomes
afraid of Macbeth. In addition, people all around begin to doubt
that anyone can be trusted. The first murder leads to many such
acts: for example, the killing of Macduff's wife and children; the
attempt to kill Banquo (which succeeds) and even his young son
Fleance (which fails). Macbeth hires murderous criminals for this
task, showing how far he has fallen from his former state, for at

an earlier stage of his life he would have had no relationship with such men, but rather would have labored to bring them to just judgment for their crimes.

6. Macbeth's loss of dominion over himself leads to a loss of dominion over his world. Scotland is compared to the garden of Eden, which is now trapped in decay. Because, like Adam in the garden, Macbeth is the king, God's vice-regent, the one in authority, the whole of his realm of Scotland is racked with wickedness and troubles. Macbeth's evil corrupts the realm. People do not know where to turn or whether there is any good left. There is a fascinating scene where one of Duncan's sons goes to England to talk to the godly king, Edward the Confessor, and Shakespeare paints a contrast between the health of the kingdom under Edward's rule and the rottenness of the Scottish state under Macbeth.

7. There is disorder even in the world of nature, for the earth is cursed because of Macbeth's sin. While he is first contemplating his murderous act, there is a dreadful storm. When the act is done, there is an immediate impact on the horses of Duncan, for they can no longer be controlled:

> And Duncan's horses, (a thing most strange and certain),
> Beauteous and swift, the minions of their race,
> Turned wild in nature, broke their stalls, flung out,
> Contending 'gainst obedience, as they would make
> War with mankind.
>   (act 2, scene 4)

Later, there are more storms and portents in the heavens. The solitary crow flies not to its own place to roost alone, but to "the rooky wood"—for, unlike crows, rooks congregate in great flocks. Horses fight and even devour each other, an act utterly against the natural order.

Shakespeare sets out in great detail the full consequences of human sin. He understands that we live in a world made by a just and righteous God, a God who cannot be mocked, a God who governs this world by his own moral character, so that the distinction between good and evil is upheld, and, whether we like it or not, evil deeds will produce evil effects. There is no escaping this, either in this life or in the life to come.

In *Macbeth* there is no echo of the story of redemption, at least where Macbeth and Lady Macbeth are concerned. Rather, for them, there is only the story of the tragedy of our human condition when we rebel against God and are unrepentant. However, there are hints of fellowship with God and of redemption in the lives of other characters and in other settings, so we are not given an utterly bleak view of the world. One example is Banquo's resisting evil because he understands that the Devil can appear to offer good things in order to entrap the human heart and to separate a person from his Creator and Redeemer:

> But 'tis strange!
> And oftentimes, to win us to our harm,
> The instruments of darkness tell us truths,
> Win us with honest trifles, to betray's
> In deepest consequence.
> (act 1, scene 3)

Another instance of hope held out by God, even for the wicked right up until the point of death, is the turning from evil of the rebellious thane of Cawdor before his execution. In words that remind the reader of the thief on the cross to whom Jesus gave the promise of everlasting life with him in Paradise, we hear of the thane's repentance, and tears come to our eyes:

> But I have spoke
> With one that saw him die, who did report
> That very frankly he confessed his treasons,
> Implored your highness' pardon, and set forth
> A deep repentance. Nothing in his life
> Became him like the leaving it. He died
> As one that had been studied in his death
> To throw away the dearest thing he owed

As 'twere a careless trifle.
>   (act 1, scene 4)

What a beautiful thing to have said about one's end! "Nothing in his life became him like the leaving of it." My father became a believer just six weeks before he died at the age of seventy-five, and so those words touch me deeply.

Other "signs" of a world in which wickedness, descent into ever-greater misery, and ultimate destruction are not the only options can be seen in the graciousness of Lady Macduff, and most especially in the life and reign of Edward the Confessor because of his delight in honoring God and serving his people in righteousness. Sadly, in many modern productions of *Macbeth*, we do not see and hear the scenes in England at Edward's court, for these are cut in the interests of shortening the play.

Measure for Measure

It is necessary to look to other plays to see Shakespeare's deep understanding of the biblical resolution to the problem of human evil. *Measure for Measure* is one play where we find a powerful and beautiful presentation of the hope there is for our lost race. This play portrays before us a moving drama of the conflict between the good use and the abuse of governing authority, of a godly approach to law or the hypocrisy of legalism, and of the need for both justice and mercy. Indeed, at the climax of *Measure for Measure* we might say, as Lewis did of the cross, that in this play's resolution, justice and mercy kiss.

I will close this essay on the echoes of Eden in Shakespeare with two brief passages about mercy from *Measure for Measure*. Both of these speeches come from Isabella when she pleads with the merciless deputy Angelo for the life of her brother Claudio, who has been condemned to death because his fiancée has become pregnant before their marriage is formalized. The second passage has a quite lovely account of Christ's work of atonement for our sins:

No ceremony that to great ones 'longs,
Not the king's crown, nor the deputed sword,
The marshal's truncheon, nor the judge's robe,
Become them with one half so good a grace
As mercy does.

    (act 2, scene 2)

Why, all the souls that were were forfeit once,
And He that might the vantage best have took
Found out the remedy. How would you be,
If He, which is the top of judgment, should,
But judge you as you are? O, think on that,
And mercy then will breathe within your lips,
Like man new-made.

    (act 2, scene 2)

10

Jane Austen,
Novelist of the Human Heart

In our final chapter we turn to a very different kind of literary work, the novels of Jane Austen. She might at first seem to have almost nothing in common with William Shakespeare, except for the obvious popularity of both writers several centuries after their works were first read. Indeed, Austen is more widely read now than at any point since her works were originally published.

Why has there been this growing popularity of Jane Austen? Is it accidental, a typical postmodern temporary fad, or is there some deeper reason for the spate of recent television series and films of Austen's novels, and the attendant increase in the sales of her books?

The Burgeoning Interest in Jane Austen

If we look back, we discover an ever-greater interest over at least the past fifty or sixty years. Indeed, we have to go back almost two generations for the first film of a Jane Austen book, the 1940 version of *Pride and Prejudice*, with Greer Garson and Laurence Olivier.

On the Republic of Pemberley website I discovered that long before I had access to a television, many productions of Austen's novels were made for TV in the 1940s, '50s, and '60s:

- *Emma* in 1948 by the BBC; in 1954 by NBC; and in 1960 by both the BBC and CBS
- *Pride and Prejudice* in 1949 by NBC; in 1952, 1958, and 1967 by the BBC

- *Sense and Sensibility* in 1950 by NBC
- *Persuasion* in 1960 by the BBC

I have not yet been able to watch any of the productions mentioned in this list.[1]

Versions I have seen are those made in the last forty years. Between 1971 and 1986 the BBC produced Jane Austen's novels for television, which are now available as a six-DVD set: *Persuasion* (1971), *Emma* (1972), *Pride and Prejudice* (1978) with Elizabeth Garvie and David Rintoul, *Sense and Sensibility* (1981), *Mansfield Park* (1983), and *Northanger Abbey* (1986).

But these very popular television series were just the firstfruits of our past generation's craze for Austen's works. Another round of versions began with the 1995 BBC production of *Persuasion*, shown on television and then released successfully in the movie theaters. It starred Amanda Root and Ciarán Hinds and was an outstanding production.

Also in 1995 *Sense and Sensibility* was released as a film, which became very popular, with Emma Thompson, Kate Winslet, and Hugh Grant. There was also the film *Clueless*, a very loose adaptation of *Emma* set in a Beverly Hills high school, with Alicia Silverstone as the Emma character.

Then a new BBC version of *Pride and Prejudice* with Colin Firth and Jennifer Ehle was aired in 1995 in Great Britain, and later in the United States, as well as many other countries. This series has been one of the most successful productions of any of the books with regard to both the numbers of viewers and the outstanding quality of the presentation. Indeed, the television drama was done excellently, with extraordinary attention to period detail as to food, flowers, clothing, furnishings, and every imaginable social custom, along with great acting in both major and minor parts and stunning locations chosen for the setting of the story.

Within a brief period two new films of *Emma* were released, the one in movie theaters, with Gwyneth Paltrow in the title role in 1996, the other, a TV film, with Kate Beckinsale in 1997.

---

[1] http://www.pemberley.com/filmography/filmography.html.

Sense and Sensibility was the most widely seen of the made-for-theater movies, setting off such large sales of the book that it was in the *New York Times* top ten fiction list for several months (along with the latest offerings of John Grisham and Tom Clancy), reaching as high as number five.

As well as the increased sales of her novels in English, these television and film versions spawned new translations of Austen's books into many languages. My French daughter-in-law, who loves good literature, had not even heard of Jane Austen in the mid-1990s. When I went with her to an excellent bookstore in Marseilles hoping to purchase French editions for her, the store manager had not heard of Austen either. But since that time, Austen's books have become widely available in French translations because of the popularity of the films. My daughter-in-law has now read all six of the novels in both French and English. She speaks of many of the characters of the books as if they were her lifelong acquaintances![2]

The BBC *Pride and Prejudice* was probably the best produced of all the adaptations so far—done not as a normal TV movie but with lavish spending to produce a five-to-six-hour feature film, shown in Britain in six episodes. There it was wildly popular with what seemed like half the nation watching it every Sunday evening (and the repeats each week on Saturdays) and then everyone talking about it at work on Mondays. Even the daily rags (sensational newspapers) had front-page articles and photographs on the state of Darcy and Elizabeth's romance week-by-week. Every bookstore in England I passed by that October had a full center-window display on Jane Austen, *Pride and Prejudice*, and the making of the film.

Finally, in this round of productions, there was a film version of *Mansfield Park* released in 1999; this was not so well done and strayed some distance from Austen's story.

Another round was kicked off in 2005 when a new production of *Pride and Prejudice* was released in the movie theaters, with the spectacularly lovely Chatsworth as Darcy's home in Derbyshire, Judi Dench as Lady Catherine de Bourgh, and Keira Knightley as

---

[2]In fact, some of Jane Austen's novels were published in French translation in the 1820s and 1830s, within a few years of their release in England.

Elizabeth Bennet. This also was very successful. The same year there was a fascinating Indian production of this same novel with the title *Bride and Prejudice*.

Andrew Davies, responsible for the great 1995 BBC *Pride and Prejudice*, made new versions of two of the novels for television in the United Kingdom: a fine presentation of *Northanger Abbey*, a 2007 Independent Television film, with J. J. Feild and Felicity Jones; and another excellent *Sense and Sensibility*, a 2008 BBC TV film, with Hattie Morahan and Charity Wakefield. Others in the ITV set were the outstanding *Persuasion*, a 2007 TV film, with Sally Hawkins and Rupert Penry-Jones, and the disappointing *Mansfield Park*, a 2007 TV film, with Billie Piper and Blake Ritson. Most recently *Emma*, in a TV miniseries produced by the BBC, has starred Romola Garai and Johnny Lee Miller.[3]

According to *Slate*, a web magazine, *Pride and Prejudice*, perhaps the best-loved of Austen's books, is now available from Amazon in 130 different editions. Even excluding academic sales, in which students have no choice but to buy the book, Nielsen BookScan calculates that *Pride and Prejudice* has sales of 110,000 a year, two hundred years after its initial publication.[4]

These figures represent more sales per year than a best seller by John Grisham within five or six years of its initial publication. As well as excluding academic sales, these figures are for the United States alone and do not include sales in the United Kingdom, or in other parts of the English-speaking world. In addition, of course, many people are downloading various editions of the book available on many different websites, and now in Kindle books. We should add that *Pride and Prejudice* and Austen's other novels have been translated into many languages and are being published both in these translations and in English all over the world. My very rough guess is that over a million copies of *Pride and Prejudice* alone are bought each year; but the true figure may be far greater still.

---

[3]For the most complete list I have found, see the website: http://www.pemberley.com/filmography/filmography.html.

[4]Adelle Waldman, "Cents and Sensibility: The Surprising Truth about Sales of Classic Novels," *Slate* (online magazine), April 2, 2003, http://www.slate.com/articles/arts/culturebox/2003/04/cents_and_sensibility.html.

Perhaps we will have to wait for the coming kingdom to know the full extent of the popularity of Austen's works in this world, if not also in the world to come.

We can sum up this brief history by concluding that many millions of people have watched and read Jane Austen's works. So, what is going on? Why is this writer—a single woman who basically lived with her family all her short life, who never traveled abroad, who writes about a very small sector of society—why is she so remarkably popular in our postmodern times?[5]

Why This Popularity?

Is it simply the beautiful dresses that the women wear? Is it a bizarre nostalgia for romanticism? (Austen was certainly not a romantic in the technical sense of this term; in fact she attacks romanticism with great passion in *Sense and Sensibility*.) Is it simply an escape from the cynicism of our postmodern age? Is it a longing for manners and courtesy, for a kinder, gentler way of relating to one another in an age of culture wars? Is it a secret interest in genuine romance to replace the cultural norm of instant sexual coupling and gratification? I mention these various options because each of them has been expressed in movie reviews and in articles about the Jane Austen "craze."

Her popularity seems to be in no danger of waning. As I mentioned in an earlier chapter, just a few years back BBC Radio conducted a poll asking women, "What book has most impacted and changed your life?" Those who organized the poll expected and hoped that the answer would be a "feminist consciousness raiser" such as Germaine Greer, *The Female Eunuch*, or *Sex and Destiny*, or at least Virginia Woolf, *To the Lighthouse*. To the pollsters' great distress, *Pride and Prejudice* won easily. The comments by the critics about this poll and its results were fascinating to read, revealing the way some intellectuals despise the reading public. The comments also showed how little some intellectuals and literary critics understand ordinary people, and how little

---

[5]Jane Austen lived just to be forty-one years old, December 16, 1775–July 18, 1817.

they understand the gifts, achievement, and even the message of Jane Austen in her novels.

To try to answer why Jane Austen is so popular today, we will look at just one of the novels here, the one that has spawned most television series and movies for the theater, *Pride and Prejudice*.[6] What is its appeal?

It is evident when one reads the book or sees any production of it that this is a deeply moral story. To give one very obvious example, this story very strongly affirms sexual chastity and rejects promiscuity. Yet, this does not appear to undermine its popularity in an age when 80 percent of high school students and well over 90 percent of college students are said to be sexually active. So, what is it that makes Jane Austen's moral vision acceptable to us, and to our postmodern contemporaries, as readers and viewers? What makes the films and television versions of *Pride and Prejudice* so popular in our relativistic age, even though it is such a profoundly moral work?

Humor

One simple answer is the humor. Austen's books are indeed hilariously funny, particularly *Pride and Prejudice*. The book has a light and sparkling appearance with its almost constant comedy and laughter. One could argue that *Mansfield Park* addresses some of the same issues as *Pride and Prejudice*—issues of sexual immorality, showing sexual promiscuity and adultery to be very serious sins—but *Mansfield Park* and the films made of it are much more challenging for our contemporaries to find acceptable. Perhaps this is because *Mansfield Park* does not have the same light and sparkling quality as *Pride and Prejudice*, and the moral failures of the characters are addressed and condemned much more directly. Many people today tend to think of Fanny Price, the heroine of *Mansfield Park*, as a self-righteous prude, though in fact she is neither self-righteous nor a prude. But she is not a cheerful, physically healthy, obviously

---

[6]If there were space here, I would gladly write about the other novels also, because my choice of *Pride and Prejudice* will disappoint some readers. Many people, my wife included, find *Persuasion* to be their favorite Austen novel. Others think of *Emma* as a perfect book. My own favorite is *Mansfield Park*, though it is the book that the film producers have least adequately presented in visual form.

sensual, or deeply amusing person in the way that we can describe Elizabeth Bennet, the heroine of *Pride and Prejudice*.

I need to add here that Austen had not lost her sense of humor when she wrote *Mansfield Park*—there is much that is amusing in it, such as one of the finest portraits of a Pharisee to appear in any English novel, shown to us in the person of Fanny's aunt Mrs. Norris. The indolence of Fanny's aunt Lady Bertram is also absurdly funny; and there are many other humorous elements to the book. But *Mansfield Park* is a very different book from *Pride and Prejudice*, for Austen did not repeat herself. Each of her six novels is a new work.

So, we may say that Austen's humor in *Pride and Prejudice* is part of the answer. Indeed, I regard *Pride and Prejudice* as the most amusing book I have ever read. I often laugh out loud when I am reading this work, no matter if it is the twentieth or thirtieth time that I have opened the book. Incidentally, Austen herself would often laugh aloud when she was writing this book, as did her family members when she "tried out" sections of the book on them by reading her developing story to them.

Austen has a sharp and amused eye for human folly and failure in all its diverse forms, and as an author she is able to capture these follies for her readers. Even her heroes and heroines ought to be laughed at, and with; and several of them have to learn their follies for themselves—like Emma Woodhouse in *Emma*, or Marianne in *Sense and Sensibility*. This delightful humor is certainly one element that helps make Austen's moral vision acceptable, even to our relativistic generation.

Related to this issue of humor is the gallery of characters in *Pride and Prejudice*. Many of these characters are very amusing, indeed unforgettable creations of Austen's imaginative genius. We will return to this issue of her creative powers later, but here I will simply say that each one of the persons who inhabits her stories is simply Austen's creation. She did not model any of her characters on people she knew—she made them up. And some of them, of course, are ridiculously absurd. Every reader or viewer probably has a favorite. The more obvious examples include Mrs. Bennet, Mr.

Collins, Mary Bennet, Sir William Lucas, Miss Bingley, and Lady Catherine de Burgh. I will say a little more about just two of these.

As we read about Mr. Collins, we see into the heart of someone who, step-by-step, becomes more and more the man he desires to be. His plan for success is to flatter the wealthy and powerful, and he justifies this ridiculous and humiliating obsequiousness as something wise and sensible. As the novel progresses, we see not just a buffoon to be laughed at, but a self-serving hypocrite to be despised very deeply; a pastor with no understanding of the gospel he professes to serve, with no love for people, and with no self-understanding. Yet, he is hilariously funny. His letters and conversation are priceless! Above all, his proposal of marriage to Elizabeth makes the reader weak with laughter at the absurdity that a man could be so unaware of his own foolishness and of the total inappropriateness of the manner in which he declares his love and asks for Elizabeth's hand. Then, within a few hours of Elizabeth's refusal of him, he has transferred his affection and admiration to Charlotte Lucas, offered himself to her, and been accepted.

Lady Catherine is presented to us as a person remarkably void of self-consciousness and filled with extraordinary self-centeredness. She lacks all charity. She loves to talk and does not require any response from those listening, except rapt attention and submission. Even her polite and respectful nephew, Colonel Fitzwilliam, acknowledges this wryly. This preposterous sense of her own worth, in comparison to the worth of the people around her, leads to the total domination of others, particularly her own poor daughter, who is crushed into anonymity by Lady Catherine's overwhelming presence.

In characters like Mr. Collins and Lady Catherine we see the brilliance of Jane Austen as a writer. She worked over her manuscripts again and again, perfecting what she wrote. She described her work in this way: "The little bit (two inches wide) of ivory on which I work with so fine a brush as to produce little effect after much labor."[7]

---

[7] Jane Austen, letter to her nephew Edward Austen-Leigh, November 1816.

The consequence of this careful labor is that every word her characters speak or write matches who they are perfectly. There is no other writer who does this so well, who has such a mastery of conversation and of the manner in which an individual's words reveal the person speaking. One could take a short excerpt from any conversation in any one of the six novels, and the speaker would be immediately identifiable. The reader who has read the novels just once could say without hesitation: "This is Miss Bates speaking; this Mr. Woodhouse; this Marianne Dashwood; this Mrs. Elton; this Mr. Collins; this Sir William Lucas; this Lady Catherine; this Mrs. Norris."

Humor and characterization come together beautifully in the novels of Jane Austen. And it is quite evident when one sees the movie or television versions that the actors are having a wonderful time playing their parts, for they are given such a clear idea of the nature of the persons whose character they inhabit and present to their audience.

There is also what we might call situation comedy, where the reader or viewer has a window into the plot and is given knowledge of the truth of people and events, knowledge that is denied to the characters in the story. Blindness to their own misperceptions creates amusing situations in *Pride and Prejudice*. I have already mentioned Mr. Collins and Lady Catherine, but we can think too of Miss Bingley, constantly misjudging Darcy's growing appreciation of Elizabeth, or her assumption that Darcy likes to be flattered, when there is nothing that he despises more. Darcy and Elizabeth, while they are the hero and heroine of the story, are constantly making errors of judgment, and this too creates humor for the reader. One example of this is Darcy's proposal to Elizabeth, though this is too painful to be really amusing!

In addition, *Pride and Prejudice* is a comedy of manners and a critique of individual and social snobbery, as well as class folly. The story is subversive and works like Jesus's parables. The humor and the ironic insight into human weaknesses and moral failure are very attractive to our hearts and minds, for we readers and viewers are invited to join Austen in her awareness of these flaws and to hold them up for our amused critique and rejection. But then we find ourselves caught up in the story and our own ironic dismissal of others' behavior, and we discover that we are on board for Austen's very serious journey of understanding into the human condition. And it may very well be that we discover in ourselves the very flaws at which we have been laughing with such enjoyment.

I have suggested that the humor and the brilliant characterization make it easier for us to be touched by the moral issues at the core of the book. What are the moral issues that are addressed in *Pride and Prejudice*?

The Moral Vices

First, there is outright immoral profligacy in a person like George Wickham. He is presented to us as a young man who, though he had an extravagant mother, was raised by an upright, hard-working, and faithful father. In addition, Wickham was well treated by his benefactor, Mr. Darcy's father. Yet, Wickham has become from his teens, and then as a matter of settled behavior, a man who is thoroughly selfish and who completely disregards what is moral, truthful, and just. He is described as "vicious" and "lacking in principle." On receiving three thousand English pounds from Darcy (an enormous amount of money two hundred years ago), in lieu of the pastoral position he has declined, he lives in "idleness and dissipation."

He is sexually without conscience and seduces women whenever he can. We read of his immoral behavior when he is a student at Cambridge. When he is in the military and stationed in Meryton, there is hardly a tradesman's daughter in Meryton who is not seduced. His running off with Lydia Bennet, the teenage daughter of a family that has treated him kindly, is the most obvious example. But whenever we see him, he is pretending love to young women simply in order to indulge himself. He does this with Elizabeth, on whom he has no serious design, as she has no money, and he sees quickly that she is committed to sexual purity and would not sleep with him. He pretends love to Miss King in order to gain access to her inheritance. He pretends love to Georgiana Darcy (when she is just sixteen) to get hold of her money.

Wickham also appears to be without any constraint or compunction when it comes to lying about other people's character and behavior. He tells appalling falsehoods about Darcy, even though Darcy was his childhood playmate, has been his benefactor, and has been extraordinarily generous to him out of respect both for his own father's wishes and for Wickham's father.

We wonder why he is so wretchedly untruthful about Darcy. We have to conclude that it is simply wickedness and malice mixed with a desire for revenge because Darcy discovered his designs on his young sister Georgiana and was able to prevent her marriage to Wickham. From that point onward he wishes to make Darcy's life unpleasant wherever he can by dishonoring his reputation and causing people to despise him. Biblically, such malicious gossip is a very serious sin, because there is a desire to destroy another person's honor and credibility; and without respect and trust from others, what place can a person have in society?

Wickham shows no remorse at any time for any of his thoroughly reprehensible behavior. Even after Darcy gives him a substantial sum of money to persuade him to marry Lydia, and when Darcy stands in as his best man, Wickham continues to dishonor Darcy and to lie about his character and actions. He even complains that Darcy is still refusing to give him a pastoral position in the church!

George Wickham, like Collins though with a great deal more success, works at being charming. He is a kind of personable rogue—"he has all the appearance of goodness, but none of the reality," as is said of him in a conversation between Jane and Elizabeth. When he and Lydia leave Longbourne, "Mr. Wickham's adieux were much more affectionate than his wife's. He smiled, looked handsome, and said many pretty things." He appears to be a man without moral conscience.

Another example of flagrant immoral behavior is that of Lydia. She is described as "the most determined flirt," and we see her throwing herself at men without any thought for the impropriety of her words and actions, or the impact they might have on an unscrupulous man, or the damage she is doing to her family's reputation in the community. Here is an account of Lydia's behavior given by Mrs. Gardiner, her aunt. This comes after Lydia has been discovered living out of wedlock with Wickham, and after Darcy has taken Lydia to live with the Gardiners until the wedding can be arranged:

> Lydia came to us; and Wickham had constant admission to the house. He was exactly what he had been when I knew him in Hertfordshire; but I would not tell you how little I was satis-fied with her behavior while she stayed with us, if I had not perceived, by Jane's letter last Wednesday, that her conduct on coming home was exactly of a piece with it, and therefore what I now tell you can give you no fresh pain. I talked to her repeatedly in the most serious manner, representing to her the wickedness of what she had done and all the unhappiness she had brought on her family. If she heard me, it was by good luck, for I am sure she did not listen. I was sometimes quite provoked, but then I recollected my dear Elizabeth and Jane, and for their sakes had patience with her.[8]

As well as depicting deceit, lies, malice, and sexual immorality in a manner that reveals their destructiveness, Austen ably captures hypocrisy, a less obvious sin, and show its ugliness. The vicar, Mr. Collins, is an appalling example of this. Austen's father was a vicar, whom she loved and admired greatly, so she understands very well the difference between genuine Christian faith and hypocrisy, between a true shepherd of Christ's flock and a fraud. She also had two brothers who were pastors, and whom she admired for their integrity and uprightness as men, husbands, fathers, and ministers carrying out their duties. In contrast to her father and brothers, Collins is presented to us as a man who has no understanding of the Christian gospel he has promised to uphold and has been ordained to serve; a pastor who has no love for the people under

---

[8] *Pride and Prejudice*, chap. 52.

his oversight; a carer of souls who has no wisdom about what it means to be responsible for the spiritual welfare of his parishioners.

He is, in some ways, a representative of a self-righteous Pharisee, for he is quick to judge people on the basis of outward behavior, but has no understanding of the evil in his own heart and conduct. Consider, for example, his letter to the Bennet family on his first hearing of Lydia's behavior, or his words to the family when he hears about the outcome of the affair between Lydia and Wickham. He is revealed to us as a man who has no business taking to himself the role of a pastor of Christ's flock. In the words below, Mr. Bennet is reading a letter from Collins. The final comment by Mr. Bennet is telling:

> "I am truly rejoiced that my cousin Lydia's sad business has been so well hushed up, and am only concerned that their living together before the marriage took place should be so generally known. I must not, however, neglect the duties of my station, or refrain from declaring my amazement, at hearing that you received the young couple into your house as soon as they were married. It was an encouragement of vice; and had I been the rector of Longbourne, I should very strenuously have opposed it. You ought certainly to forgive them, as a Christian, but never to admit them in your sight, or allow their names to be mentioned in your hearing." That is his notion of Christian forgiveness![9]

Collins is also a flatterer of the worst sort, a man with absurd obsequiousness to those who are above him in society's hierarchy. Again, this is completely out of place in one who is supposed to be representing Christ to people; one who is supposed to be no respecter of persons; one who is called to welcome even the smallest child; one who is to speak against sin wherever it is found, including among the wealthy and powerful. None of these requisite characteristics are found in Collins's life or words; rather, the exact opposite. Every word and every action is suited to serve his

---

[9]*Pride and Prejudice*, chap. 57.

own advantage and to curry favor for himself with the wealthy and powerful in his own parish and elsewhere.

Marriage is held in high honor by Jane Austen, and *Pride and Prejudice* is full of reflections about what constitutes a wise and good marriage. Charlotte's mistaken views of marriage are treated as a moral issue. For Charlotte a good marriage is a matter of chance. She believes one cannot truly know another person until you live with that person. So, her approach to marriage is purely practical: a woman needs a husband who can support her and provide her a home. But the consequence she quickly discovers is that her marriage to Mr. Collins is made tolerable only by spending as little time with him as possible, and by choosing not to hear much of what he says.

This failure of Charlotte's approach to marriage raises the moral issue of the fundamental need for respect and true affection between husband and wife. This is addressed repeatedly and with very great care: regarding Lydia and Wickham, Jane and Bingley, Mr. and Mrs. Bennet, and above all Elizabeth and Darcy. Jane sums up this attitude in her words to Elizabeth when she hears of her engagement to Darcy: "Do anything rather than marry without affection." We should also note here Mr. Bennet's words: "My child, let me not have the grief of seeing you unable to respect your partner in life."

In *Pride and Prejudice* Austen presents husband and wife as moral and intellectual equals—that is her ideal, and it is clearly the teaching of Scripture. We see this in the developing relationship between Elizabeth and Darcy; though we should also notice that each of these two thinks of the other as the superior, which is what genuinely Christian love and a Christian approach to marriage require of us.

The need for respect between husband and wife is discussed at length in the account of Mr. Bennet's treatment of his wife. Though in many respects he is a man to be liked and admired, yet in his marriage, he fails to honor his wife, and holds her up for ridicule to her own children.

Had Elizabeth's opinion been drawn all from her own family, she could not have formed a very pleasing picture of conjugal felicity or domestic comfort. Her father, captivated by youth and beauty, and that appearance of good humor which youth and beauty generally give, had married a woman whose weak understanding and illiberal mind had very early in their marriage put an end to all real affection for her. Respect, esteem, and confidence had vanished for ever; and all his views of domestic happiness were overthrown. But Mr. Bennet was not of a disposition to seek comfort for the disappointment which his own imprudence had brought on, in any of the pleasures which too often console the unfortunate for their folly or their vice. He was fond of the country and of books; and from these tastes had arisen his principal enjoyments. To his wife he was very little otherwise indebted, than as her ignorance and folly had contributed to his amusement. This was not the sort of happiness which a man would in general wish to owe to his wife but where other means of entertainment are wanting, the true philosopher will derive benefit from such as are given.

Elizabeth, however, had never been blind to the impropriety of her father's behavior as a husband. She had always seen it with pain; but respecting his abilities, and grateful for his affectionate treatment of herself, she endeavored to forget what she could not overlook, and to banish from her thoughts that continual breach of conjugal obligation and decorum which, in exposing his wife to the contempt of her own children, was so highly reprehensible. But she had never felt so strongly as now the disadvantages which must attend the children of so unsuitable a marriage, nor ever been so fully aware of the evils arising from so ill-judged a direction of talents; talents which, if rightly used, might at least have preserved the respectability of his daughters, even if incapable of enlarging the mind of his wife.[10]

Along with the failure to honor his wife, Mr. Bennet is held up for our criticism because of his neglect of his responsibilities as a father. He is shown to have given himself to the intellectual and moral education of his two older daughters, Jane and Elizabeth;

---

[10]*Pride and Prejudice*, chap. 42.

but it is apparent that he has given up after that point and abandoned the three younger daughters to their own whims and to their mother. Basically he has allowed the girls to raise themselves; and he has left his wife to shape their minds and hearts, though he knows she is incapable of doing this wisely.

He allows Kitty and Lydia to drift in life without any moral or spiritual input from him, their father. Indeed, he laughs at these two and Mary, and refers to them as three of the silliest girls in England. The consequences are disastrous in Mary, even though she seems better educated than Kitty and Lydia. She is constantly reading, though without discernment or wisdom; she works hard at the piano and singing, but her musical accomplishment is slight, her knowledge merely technical, her understanding of music poor; and her lack of awareness of the severe limitations of her gifts is pitiable. Unlike Lydia and Kitty she is not a flirt. Yet, in truth, she is just as self-centered as Kitty and Lydia. She is pretentious and even proud of her ideas and herself without reason.

The consequences are also disastrous for Kitty, and worst of all for Lydia, for Lydia is the one most like her mother, and therefore the one most spoiled and most indulged by Mrs. Bennet. In these three younger girls we see the absence of good parenting held up as folly that certainly makes us laugh; but even more than the humor, and brought into clearer focus by the humor, what we see is parental neglect that is deeply reprehensible.

Another moral issue revealed for our ridicule is the social snobbery of Miss Bingley and Mrs. Hurst, two of the most prominent examples of this evil among the many in the book (Lady Catherine being another). They have no regard for the true happiness of their brother, Charles Bingley, or for the obvious moral virtues of Jane Bennet, with whom Charles is deeply in love. Miss Bingley is a woman who never thinks about deep moral questions and who cares only about social position, appearance, wealth, and her own advantage. It is fascinating to observe Miss Bingley's response to the Gardiners: her reaction on discovering that the Gardiners live in Cheapside (an unfashionable district in London); her disdain when she hears about Mr. Gardiner's means of livelihood as a business man (though her own family's fortune came originally through trade); and her insufferable rudeness and coldness when she visits Jane in the Gardiners' home—and then to contrast her response and the response of Darcy when he meets Mr. and Mrs. Gardiner; when he spends time in their home without any apparent thought that he is moving beneath himself socially; when he treats them with the deepest respect and kindness.

Mrs. Bennet is portrayed as another person who lacks deep moral reflection and conviction. She is interested in marriages of money and status for her elder daughters, and for the way such marriages will reflect on her. For her younger daughters she desires merely that they will have fun, and gives no thought to the propriety or wisdom of their behavior. Mrs. Bennet is judged and found wanting as a parent, though we expect nothing better from her because of her own lack of moral sensitivity, her own self-centeredness, and her foolishly romantic and yet sometimes totally pecuniary approach to her daughters' prospects of marriage.

Mrs. Bennet is a deeply selfish woman and a foolish woman (in the sense of the "foolish woman" of Proverbs), one who has no sense of her own folly. She is able to forget immoral behavior instantly; and this is very different from realizing its seriousness and forgiving it. Her life appears to revolve entirely around what makes her happy. She makes no effort to understand her husband, to truly honor him, or to serve him; and she has no understanding of what it means to raise her children rightly. As an example of her self-centeredness and insensitivity, observe her lack of appreciation for her brother's kindness to her family, when Mr. and Mrs. Gardiner do so much to help Lydia. Mrs. Bennet takes their generosity for granted, as if such self-sacrifice were her right, and she dismisses Jane and Elizabeth's attempts to convince her of how indebted they are to the Gardiners, and how truly grateful the whole Bennet family ought to be.

Many other examples of moral failure are held up both for derision and condemnation—and we should note again that the humor dancing through the book makes such moral passion acceptable in our cultural setting, for *Pride and Prejudice* is not a sermon or a moral treatise!

The Moral Virtues

But what about moral virtues—which of these are cherished and held up for our delight?

Respect and honor for one's parents are presented to us as thoroughly admirable. Here both Jane and Lizzie shine as examples. Despite the many flaws in their parents, particularly their mother, they are unfailingly polite and respectful in their presence and when speaking about them. They maintain this respect even when they finally feel the need to express problems, for example, when Elizabeth talks to her father about his failure to restrain Lydia.

Fairness and generosity to those who are under one socially are shown to be thoroughly praiseworthy, and also rare; for Austen recognizes that most people with money, status, and power get carried away only with their own interests. In this regard Darcy is a paragon of virtue. He is viewed with the greatest respect by those who have worked in his house and on his estate. A man who is well spoken of by those under him is indeed a good man. There are very few such men in this world.

Basic decency, kindness, and a willingness to give oneself to the service of others are virtues held up for our praise. Here Elizabeth and Jane and the Gardiners are portrayed as always ready to serve and to give of themselves unstintingly to other people.

Readiness to resist intimidation by people's social standing and wealth is also set forth for us to approve. Consider the example of Elizabeth in the presence of Darcy's aunt, Lady Catherine de Burgh, both when Elizabeth visits in the aunt's home and when Lady Catherine comes to the Bennet home to forbid Elizabeth to marry Darcy. Elizabeth is courteous and polite, but never intimidated into submission or subservience by Lady Catherine's wealth, power, and dominating personality.

Gentleness of spirit is shown for our delight in the person of Jane. She is a portrait of the qualities of love as set out by the apostle Paul in 1 Corinthians 13. Jane is patient and kind; she is not envious or boastful; she is not arrogant or rude; she does not insist on her own way; she is not irritable or resentful; she does not rejoice in wrongdoing, but rejoices with the truth. Jane bears all things, believes all things, hopes all things, endures all things. Her love never fails. Jane even seeks to forgive Miss Bingley and to treat her well. One of the remarkable achievements of Austen is to present Jane as a lovable and delightful person. We saw earlier that it is remarkably difficult to present goodness in an attractive way (see Lewis's introduction to *The Screwtape Letters*). However, Jane is a thoroughly likable person. She does not sparkle like Elizabeth, but Elizabeth herself understands that some of her sparkling has to do with not entirely positive qualities in her own makeup.

Love is revealed as a readiness to forgive and to accept, even when deep wrong has been done. Jane and Elizabeth manage to persuade their father to welcome Lydia and Wickham to Long-bourne after their marriage, and clearly this is presented to us as the nature of genuine Christian forgiveness—which indeed it is.

Pride and Prejudice presents a biblical approach to marriage. If we look at the relationship between Elizabeth and Darcy as an example, we find the growth of mutual honor and respect. We also find a growing gentleness and even submissive spirit in Elizabeth toward Darcy, once she understands his true worth and begins to love him; though this will never become a servile submission on her part, for, rightly, she regards herself as his human equal.

In Darcy, once he is humbled and comes to a more appropriate estimate of himself and of Elizabeth, we find a husband ready to love and serve his wife in whatever ways he can, even if it means rejection by family members and friends. Many people in his day would have looked down not only on the whole Bennet family after Lydia's disgrace, but also on anyone who allied themselves with the girls of the Bennet family in marriage. This issue clearly has no power over him. He loves Elizabeth for who she is, regardless of her family connections. This is one way in which he changes so dramatically. The issue of her social status is at the front of his mind when he first proposes to her. Once he has been humbled and has come to a far deeper realization of Elizabeth's worth, he puts such arrogance away entirely; and from that point on he thinks of her family with respect and even deep honor.

Darcy is prepared to humble himself, even to humiliate himself, for the sake of Elizabeth, to serve her and to do good to Lydia. He seeks out Mrs. Younge even though such an effort must be miserable for him (given her duplicity when she was chaperone for Darcy's sister Georgiana at the time of Wickham's attempt to entice her into eloping with him). Darcy gives this woman money so that she will reveal to him the whereabouts of Lydia and Wickham. He gives Wickham a substantial amount of money so that he will consent to marry Lydia; and he even acts as the best man and witness at the wedding to make sure that Wickham makes it to the altar. And Darcy does all this for a man he has every reason to hate, despise, and wish never to see again.

In effect Darcy buys this wretched man to be his own future brother-in-law, though at the point he does all this, he has no confidence that he can persuade Elizabeth to love him. Austen gives us here an example of what Paul means when he says a husband is to love his wife as Christ loved the church: he loved her and gave himself for her (Ephesians 5). Darcy humbles himself in a multitude of lovely ways. He declares to the Gardiners that it is his mistaken pride that has caused people to be taken in by Wickham, his unwillingness to lay his own life and troubles bare before the world. Darcy becomes, during the course of the novel, a man of humility, grace, and moral beauty.

Pride and Prejudice constantly touches deep moral chords in the human soul. The book and the films teach the importance of self-control, courtesy, a mannerly consideration for others, humility, love, kindness and generosity, respect and honor—and many other virtues. But these virtues are presented not simply as pleasant social behavior that will make society run more smoothly, but as truly moral characteristics—ones that arise from the profound sense of a Christian moral order pervading this book and all of Jane Austen's novels. We are invited to love what is good, what is kind, what is just, what is merciful and faithful. And we are invited to laugh at, and to loathe, what is unfaithful, dishonest, selfish, proud, and mean.

Perhaps the deepest issues of all that are dealt with in this book are the importance of personal humility, the readiness to see one's weaknesses and failings, and then to desire to change. This is true for the two central characters of the book, Darcy and Elizabeth. They both come to the realization that they have been guilty of pride and prejudice. Here are Darcy's words about his learning that he was a proud, self-centered, and ungracious man:

> Painful recollections will intrude, which cannot, which ought not, to be repelled. I have been a selfish being all my life, in practice, though not in principle. As a child, I was taught what was right: but I was not taught to correct my temper. I was given good principles, but left to follow them in pride and conceit. Unfortunately, an only son (for many years an only child), I was spoiled by my parents, who, though good themselves, (my father particularly, all that was benevolent and amiable), allowed, encouraged, almost taught me to be selfish and overbearing—to care for none beyond my own family circle, to think meanly of the rest of the world, to wish at least to think meanly of their sense and worth compared to my own. Such I was, from eight to eight-and-twenty; and such I might still have been but for you, dearest, loveliest Elizabeth! What do I not owe you? You taught me a lesson, hard indeed at first, but most advantageous. By you I was properly humbled.

He adds that he cannot think of his first proposal without "abhorrence" at his attitude and behavior on that occasion; he cannot think of them without it being "inexpressibly painful" to himself. He acknowledges that the letter he composed, after her refusal of his proposal, was written in "dreadful bitterness of spirit" and that it would be quite "just" of Elizabeth to "hate" him for it. There are few examples in fiction, and even fewer in life, of men speaking with such frank and wise humility about themselves. For men of Darcy's social standing and wealth, in his day or in our day, such attitudes are truly rare. It is such moral loveliness as this that makes *Pride and Prejudice* such a joy to read.

Here is a man prepared to be humbled by a proper rebuke from the woman he loves and to seek to learn from it: "... to show you by every civility in my power, that I hoped to obtain your forgiveness, to lessen your ill-opinion by letting you see that your reproofs had been attended to." Then come this description and Elizabeth's words after she has read Darcy's letter and discovered that she has been guilty of the worst kind of blind prejudice:

> She grew absolutely ashamed of herself. Of neither Darcy nor Wickham could she think without feeling that she had been blind, partial, prejudiced, absurd.
>
> "How despicably I have acted!" she cried; "I, who have prided myself on my discernment! I, who have valued myself on my abilities! Who have often disdained the generous candor of my sister, and gratified my vanity in useless or blamable mistrust. How humiliating is this discovery! Yet, how just a humiliation! Had I been in love, I could not have been more wretchedly blind. But vanity, not love, has been my folly. Pleased by the preference of one, and offended by the neglect of the other, on the very beginning of our acquaintance, I have courted prepossession and ignorance, and driven reason away, where either were concerned. Till this moment I never knew myself."

These two accounts of the humbling of Darcy and Elizabeth are among the finest expressions I have found of a genuinely Christian understanding of personal humility and repentance. Austen was a deeply committed Christian, and a Christian moral order and understanding of the human heart pervade her novels. Yet, we have to marvel that these novels, so filled with a Christian moral vision, are gladly embraced by our postmodern generation.

This is a miracle, and in seeking to explain this phenomenon I have spoken of Jane Austen's humor, of the romance, of the characterization, and of the care she gives to speech patterns. We could add many other qualities that make Austen a great writer. One of the greatest is the full development of character that she brings to her stories, including the way the main characters mature and develop as the stories progress. The people in her novels live for us. We get to know them. We imagine meeting them and having conversations with them. We may even dream about them. We want to know what happens to them after the story finishes. They become our friends.

Both in Austen's day and in ours, critics and readers have been so taken by this realism in her portrayal of her characters that they have assumed she was writing about herself and people she knew. It is this realism that has led many writers to try to discover Austen's own life and her own history of romance from her novels. In particular, many have assumed that the remarkably acute portrayal of Anne Elliot in *Persuasion* must be a reflection of Austen's own personal experience. One can repeatedly find such statements as this: "Through Anne Elliot's smiles, we may discern Jane Austen's tears."

Austen was offended by such responses, and she insisted that she simply made up her characters, creating them out of her own imagination. I close by revisiting Elizabeth Jenkins's wonderful words about this quality of Jane Austen's creative genius, words in which Jenkins compares Austen's ability to create character to the accomplishment of William Shakespeare:

> To try to deduce from Jane Austen's novels a personal history of Jane Austen, is completely to misunderstand the type of mind she represents.
>
> The creative mind of the first order is infinitely difficult to understand; Dryden understood it when he said of Shakespeare: "After God, he has created most"; but there are numberless people who say "Anne Elliot *must* be Jane Austen" because Jane Austen could never have otherwise understood how Anne Elliot would have felt; and the only thing that deters them from believing that Shakespeare smothered his wife in a fit of jealousy, was deeply distressed by a second marriage of his mother's, murdered a distinguished guest in the hope of succeeding him in his office, and was finally turned out of doors by his ungrateful children, is that the stories of Othello, Hamlet, Macbeth and Lear were published and widely known before he undertook them.

The highest type of creative genius owes to daily life at once everything and nothing; its implements, its medium, are supplied by observation of the topical existence, but its inspiration lies in the fact that owing to some extraordinary *lusus naturae* it is in touch with something that encompasses us but that the rest of us do not see; racial memory or basic consciousness, one knows not how to name this vantage ground, and dark as it is to us, there is no doubt that it was equally so to the conscious mind of its possessors. But when they postulated to themselves a human being in a particular situation, something nameless whispered to them all the rest. How could Shakespeare, three hundred years before anyone had investigated the working of the sub-conscious mind, have understood that though Lady Macbeth had urged her husband not to be appalled by blood, which a little water could wash away, yet when her conscious mind was asleep, she was haunted by the nightmare that she would never get the bloodstains off her hands?

When Macaulay mentioned Shakespeare and Jane Austen in the same breath, he did not suppose it necessary to state the obvious difference in their art and scope; admirers of Jane Austen understood what he meant in making the comparison, and feel that however far apart they stand, the two share the quality, in however differing degrees, of creating character.

It is this most unusual caliber of mind that she possessed which is the inmost secret of her skill and explains, in so far as words can explain, the miracle of her achievement.[11]

---

[11]Elizabeth Jenkins, *Jane Austen* (London: Sphere, 1972), 64.

Appendix

The "Outing" of Dumbledore

It might be helpful to some readers for me to make a few comments about Rowling's statement in the fall of 2007 that Dumbledore is gay. Earlier in the chapter on Harry Potter I referred to Dumbledore's troubled youth and his friendship with a young wizard from the Continent. It is this young man, Gellert Grindelwald, for whom Dumbledore has a gay passion, Rowling has said. However, it should be noted that there is no hint of this in the book, and the comment may be completely disregarded by the reader. Albus Dumbledore does not come across as gay in the story. He does not claim to be gay. No one else suggests that he is gay, in either a positive or a negative way. He clearly has a passionate friendship with the golden-haired, laughing, and handsome young man, but there is not the slightest suggestion in the book of sexual involvement between the two.

For the reader it is important not to let this issue determine how to think about the books. Indeed, once an author has written her work, she has no right to suggest or demand an interpretation that the text itself does not support. This "outing" is merely a distraction, and my own guess is that Rowling made this statement in response to criticism after the publication of this final book. Much to the surprise of Christians who had damned the books as being immoral, some secular writers declared that the books are bourgeois and have characters with a too traditional morality.

Some of the critics attacked the last book because they were distressed by her final section, which shows the chief characters Harry and Ginny, Ron and Hermione, nineteen years later, happily married to each other and living a settled life, with well-adjusted, happy children. This was too much for some of the critics to stomach! That particular assault has gone quiet after Rowling's remark that Dumbledore is gay. In the context, she was answering a question from one member of a packed audience at Carnegie Hall. People gave her sustained applause. But her words, I think, are merely a distraction, which the liberal and gay communities have grasped at like a drowning man grasps a straw.

There is an irony in this, and it seems to me a delicious irony that has passed those critics by who have been so euphoric about Rowling's words on Dumbledore's gay passion. Their argument has been that for such a central character to have been gay is a great encouragement to homosexuals. The irony is this: if anything is clear in this book, it is that Dumbledore's life at that stage is not to be emulated; far from it, in fact. He himself weeps over his thinking and behavior at that stage of his life, in particular over his relationship with Grindelwald, and he is shown to be deeply penitent and full of remorse. He knows he needs forgiveness for the way he has lived, and he spends his life thereafter seeking to bear fruits worthy of repentance. I have a suspicion that J. K. Rowling may be laughing up her sleeve over this matter—but do not expect her to "come out" publicly and acknowledge the comedy.

General Index

abstract art, 51–52
Aeschylus, 157
alienation, 74, 161, 162
allegory, 109, 118
alternative universe, 128, 133–34
Anglo-Saxon, 108, 110
Antony and Cleopatra, 151–52
Apollo, 80–81
Aragon (character), 43, 122–23
Aratus, 76–77
arrogance, 56
art
  Christians on, 11, 37, 39–42
  and community, 22
  creation, fall, redemption in, 43
  as didactic and evangelistic, 41
  as divine calling, 55
  as honest, 45
  as imitative, 23–27
  needs no justification, 22, 37, 41
  by non-Christians, 31–34
  traditions of, 57
  and truth, 67
  as worldly, 37
"art for art's sake," 37
artisans, 34–35
arts and crafts, 34–37
asceticism, 17–18
Aslan (character), 46, 99, 102–3
Athenians, 76–78
atonement, 75, 167
Augustine, 25, 88
Austen, Jane, 35, 169–92
  humor of, 174–78
  integrity as artist, 62
  popularity of, 36, 58–59, 169–74

Babel, 73
Babylon, 83
Bach, J. S., 27, 34
Bacon, Francis, 26
baptism, 51
Barr, Donald, 113
BBC, 36, 173
  productions of Jane Austen, 170, 171
Beckinsale, Kate, 170
Beethoven, Ludwig von, 41
Beowulf, 105–6, 110
biographies, 44
Blake, William, 46
blasphemy, in movies and literature, 59–60
bodily resurrection, 19
Branagh, Kenneth, 149
Bride and Prejudice, 172
brokenness, 43, 74–75, 116
Browne, Thomas, 91
Buddhism, 92

Cage, John, 58
callings, 22
Calvin, John
  on common grace, 32–33, 54
  on creation, 12–13, 17, 68–70
  on reading classics, 136–37
Calvinism, on the arts, 55
carnal, art as, 37
Carpenter, Humphrey, 93
characters
  of Harry Potter series, 129
  in Jane Austen, 175–78, 190–91
cherubim, 47
Chesterton, G. K., 91

Child, Lee, 36
children
   play imaginative games, 128,
      133–34
   start serious reading through
      Harry Potter, 125, 129
Christian art, 39–42
Christians, attacks on Harry Potter
   series, 125–26
Chronicles of Narnia, The (Lewis),
   50, 96
   as alternative universe, 128
   "echoes of Eden" in, 99–104
   occult in, 133, 135
Churchill, Winston, 147
Clancy, Tom, 171
class folly, 177
classics, 136
Clueless (film), 170
Cold War, 115
collective unconsciousness, 79
comedy of manners, 177
common grace, 19, 32–33
communism, 115
courage, 106
Covenant Theological Seminary,
   55–56
crafts, 34–37
creation, 16–19, 68–70
   in Harry Potter series, 131
   in *The Lord of the Rings*, 119–20
creativity
   of artist, 26
   of Shakespeare, 154–55
   of unbelievers, 32
criteria, for judging the arts, 54–64
culture, Christian response to,
   136–38
cursing, in movies and literature, 59

David, 20, 44
Davies, Andrew, 172

da Vinci, Leonardo, 35
death
   as last enemy, 138, 145
   in *The Lord of the Rings*, 117, 121
decency, 186
Dench, Judi, 148, 171
De Quincey, Thomas, 30
development, of artistic gifts, 55–56
Devil, 82–84, 100
DiCaprio, Leonardo, 149
Diogenes Laërtius, 77
discernment, 53, 132
diversity, of creation, 15
dominion, 20–21, 22, 133
Domitian (Emperor), 80
Donne, John, 27, 45, 91
Dowling, W. C., 117–18
dragon, 80, 82–83
drama, 51
Dryden, John, 23, 191
Dumbledore, Albus (character), 139,
   141–42, 145
   "outing" of, 193–94
Dyson, Hugo, 93

"echoes of Eden," 43, 74
   in Harry Potter series, 131
   in literature, 79
   in *The Lord of the Rings*, 124
   in mythological stories, 83
   in Narnia stories, 99–104
   in Shakespeare, 156
Eden, original glory of, 26
Egypt, 80, 83
Ehle, Jennifer, 170
Eliot, T. S., 27, 31, 45, 61
elitism, 64, 65
Ellington, Duke, 35
Elliot, Anne (character), 191
Emma, 169, 170, 172, 174n6, 175
enjoyment, of creation, 16–19
entertainment, art as, 63–64

Epimenides, 76–77
"equalizing heresy," 65
eternity, in our hearts, 88
Euripedes, 157
evangelism, art as, 41
evil
    in art, 60–61
    Lewis on, 120
    in *The Lord of the Rings*, 115–17,
       119–21
    in *Macbeth*, 156–59, 160, 163–64
    in Narnia stories, 100–101
ex nihilo, 20

fairness, 186
fairy stories
    Lewis on, 88
    Tolkien on, 81
fall, 16, 29, 58, 74, 161
    in *The Lord of the Rings*, 120
    in Narnia stories, 100–101
    setting back boundaries of, 22
    as subject for artist, 43
fantasy, suspicions of, 126, 127,
    132–35
Feild, J. J., 172
fiction, 31, 116
films
    of Jane Austen, 169–72
    of Shakespeare, 149
fine art, 34–35
Firth, Colin, 170
Fishburne, Lawrence, 149
flattery, in *Pride and Prejudice*, 181
form and content, 61
Free University of Amsterdam, 34
fulfillment, as calling, 22

Garai, Romola, 172
Garvie, Elizabeth, 170
general revelation, 67–74
generosity, 186, 188

gentleness of spirit, 186–87
Germanic languages, 108
Germanic myths, 117
giftedness, 54–55, 66
glory of God, 22, 27, 56
God
    as Creator, 11–16, 58
    as "distant king" in *The Lord of the
      Rings*, 119
    as enemy in *Macbeth*, 161–62
    metaphors for, 42, 48
    as ruler over nations, 72–74
good and evil
    in alternative universe, 135
    in Harry Potter series, 130–31, 144
goodness
    of creation, 19, 119–20
    in *The Lord of the Rings*, 119–20
gospel, as greatest fairy story, 81,
    93–94
Gospels, Lewis on, 92
gossip, 136
Gothic, 108, 110
grace, general and special, 33
Grant, Hugh, 170
Greece, 80
Greek tragedy, 160
Greer, Germaine, 36, 173
Greeves, Arthur, 89, 93
Grisham, John, 171, 172

Haggard, H. Rider, 64
hagiographies, 44
Hamlet, 58, 155
Harry Potter and the Deathly Hallows,
    138–39
Harry Potter series, 124–45
    good and evil in, 130–31
    value of, 127–32
heart, 65
hedonism, 37
Herbert, George, 18, 23, 45, 91

heroism, in Tolkien, 106, 121–22
high culture, 34
Hinds, Ciarán, 170
Hindu tragedy, 160
Hiram, King of Tyre, 32
Hitler, Adolf, 115, 147
Hobbit, The, 118, 133
hobbits, as heroes, 121–22
holiness, 91, 120
Holy Spirit, 136–37
homosexuals, 193–94
honor, 186, 188
hope
    in *The Lord of the Rings*, 121
    in Narnia stories, 101
Hopkins, Anthony, 61
Hopkins, Gerard Manley, 13–14, 45,
    100
humanists, on Tolkien and Lewis,
    117
human nature, as revelation, 70
human significance, in *Macbeth*,
    159–60
humility, 23, 28, 56, 121–22
    in *Pride and Prejudice*, 187–88,
    189–90
humor, in Jane Austen, 174–78
hypocrisy, 60, 180–81

idolatry, 46, 48, 81
image of God
    and creation of alternative uni-
        verse, 133–34
    and sub-creators, 19–22
imagination, 48, 91, 133–34
    of J. K. Rowling, 128
imitation of Christ, 24
incarnation, 19
integrity
    of artist, 62–63
    in work of art, 63

"intimations of immortality," 88,
    123
inventiveness, 16
Islam, 46, 73

James, P. D., 36
Jenkins, Elizabeth, 154–55, 191–92
Jesus Christ
    as fulfillment of vestiges of truth
        in myths, 81
    as fully human, 45
    incarnation of, 47, 49–50, 51
    as storyteller, 96
Job, blasphemy in, 59
Johnson, Samuel, 31, 91
Jones, Felicity, 172
joy, Lewis on, 87, 88–89, 91
Joyce, James, 36, 113
Julius Caesar, 153
Jung, Carl, 79

Kalevala, The, 111
Khomeini, Ayatollah, 73
kindness, 186, 188
Knightley, Keira, 171
Kuyper, Abraham, 54–55

L'Abri Fellowship, 34
Lang, Andrew, 110
Langland, William, 91
laziness, 56
Lecter, Hannibal (character), 60–61
Lee, Christopher, 114
legends, 79
Leviathan, 82–83
Lewis, C. S., 64
    on artist as imitator, 24–25
    on Christian literature, 39–40
    conversion of, 94–95, 105
    on "equalizing heresy," 65
    on evil, 120
    on fantasy, 134–35

on giftedness, 66
on great art and artists, 21, 28
humanists on, 117
on longing for God, 88
on *The Lord of the Rings*, 116,
    134–35
Narnia stories, 46, 50
on Psalm 119, 12
on reading, 28–31
on sub-creation, 26
on Tolkien, 107
on writing, 97–98
Lewis, Warren, 85–86
Liddell, Eric, 56
Lion, the Witch, and the Wardrobe,
    The, 96, 99–104
literature, 30–31, 39–40, 79
Loizeaux, Daniel, 14
Longfellow, Henry Wadsworth, 86
Lord of the Rings, The, 43, 105–24
    characters of, 114
    as myth not allegory, 109, 118
    no mention of religion, 117–18
    occult in, 133, 135
    popularity of, 112–24
    realism of, 115–17
Lord's Supper, 47, 51
love
    for God, 29
    in *The Lord of the Rings*, 119
    for neighbor, 29
    in *Pride and Prejudice*, 187, 188
    in Tolkien, 106
Luther, Martin, 147
Lystra, 78

Macbeth, 58, 156–67
MacDonald, George, 89–91, 95, 110
"mannishness of man," 70
Mansfield Park, 170, 171, 172, 174–75
Marlowe, Christopher, 153
marriage, Jane Austen on, 182, 187

marriage supper of the Lamb, 47
Marx, Karl, 147
Mary, mother of Jesus, 49
Measure for Measure, 167–68
meekness, 121–22
memories, 74–75
Mesopotamia, 80
Michelangelo, 35
Middle-earth, 26, 107, 109, 111–15,
    118, 122, 124, 128
Middle English, 108, 110
Midsummer Night's Dream, A, 148–49
Miller, Johnny Lee, 172
Milton, John, 91
Mirren, Helen, 149
Morahan, Hattie, 172
moral complexity, of Harry Potter
    series, 131
moral goodness, in art, 59–61
moral greatness, versus giftedness,
    66
moral vices, in *Pride and Prejudice*,
    178–86
moral virtues, in *Pride and Prejudice*,
    186–90
Morris, William, 111
Mother Teresa, 147
museums, 35
Muslims, 73
Mythopoeia, 94, 105, 118
myth
    versus allegory, 109, 118
    Tolkien on, 93–95
    truth in, 80–81, 107

name of God, misuse of, 60
Narnia stories. *See The Chronicles of*
    Narnia
Nazis, 115
Nebuchadnezzar, 73
new creation, 19
new heavens and new earth, 48

new life, 99
Newton, Isaac, 20–21
non-Christian art, 31–34
Norse myths, 117
Northanger Abbey, 170, 172
nuclear weapons, 115
nudity, in art, 60

occult, 132, 135–36, 144
O'Connor, Flannery, 55, 116
Oedipus Rex, 157
old creation, as contaminated, 16
Old English, 108
Old Norse, 108, 110
originality, of artist, 26
other-centeredness, 56–57
Oxford, 111

Pacino, Al, 149
paganism, myths and idols of,
    80–81
Paltrow, Gwyneth, 170
Paradise, 26
    lost in *The Lord of the Rings*, 120
    regained in *The Lord of the Rings*,
    124
parallelism, 42
parenting, Jane Austen on, 183–84
parents, respect and honor for, 186
Passover, 51
Paul
    on asceticism, 17–18
    on human nature, 70–71
    on Mars Hill, 73–75, 76–78
    on providential care, 72
Pausanias, 77
Pearl, The (poem), 110
Penry-Jones, Rupert, 172
Perelandra, 94, 95
perfection, of creation, 14–15
Persuasion, 170
philology, 111

Piers Plowman (poem), 110
Piper, Billie, 172
Plato, 136
Platonic view of arts, 25
playwrights, 97
Plotinus, 25
poetry, 41–42, 86–87, 110
    of Shakespeare, 151–52, 160
Polanski, Roman, 157
pornography, 60
postmodern age, 57, 58, 169, 173
Potter, Beatrix, 134
power, 121
prayer, 162
preaching, integrity of, 62–63
Pride and Prejudice, 26, 169, 170,
    171–72, 173, 174–90
profusion, of creation, 15
propaganda, 58
prophets
    use of drama, 51
    use of mythology, 82–84
providential care, 19, 71–72, 74, 78
psalms, Lewis on, 91
Pullman, Phillip, 117

qualities
    of art, 53
    of good literature, 39–40
Quenya (elvish language), 111, 115

Rackham, Arthur, 88
rainbow, 51
reading, 28–31
reading aloud, 114
realism
    in *The Lord of the Rings*, 115–17
    of Jane Austen, 191
rebellious attitude toward authority,
    126–27
redemption
    as fit material for artist, 43

in Harry Potter series, 131
in *The Lord of the Rings*, 121, 123
in *Macbeth*, 166–67
in Narnia stories, 101–3
as new creation, 19
religion, missing in *The Lord of the Rings*, 117–18
Rembrandt, 27, 34, 46, 50–51
Renaissance, 35
repentance, in *Pride and Prejudice*, 190
representational art, 45–51
respect, 186, 188
resurrection, of Aslan, 102–3
Revelation, use of legends in, 79–84
Richardson, Don, 76
Rintoul, David, 170
Ritson, Blake, 172
Roman Catholicism, of Tolkien, 109
Romanticism, 27–28, 34, 36–37, 173
Romeo and Juliet, 147–48
Rookmaaker, Hans, 34
Roosevelt, Franklin D., 147
Root, Amanda, 170
Rousseau, Jean-Jacques, 25
Rowling, J. K., 126–32, 135–36, 137–38, 142
as Christian believer, 137, 144–45
on Dumbledore, 193–94

sacraments, 47–48
sacred-secular distinction, 21
sacrifice, 51, 75. *See also* self-sacrifice
Satan, 82–83, 100
Sayers, Dorothy, 97
Schaeffer, Francis, 58, 70
Scotland, compared to Eden in *Macbeth*, 165
second commandment, and representational art, 45–51
secular vocations, 21
self-centeredness, 56–57, 132

self-control, 188
self-destruction, in *Macbeth*, 163
self-expressive art, 27–28
selfishness, 185
self-sacrifice
of Aslan, 102
in *Beowulf*, 106
in Harry Potter series, 131–32, 138–45
in *The Lord of the Rings*, 119, 123
in Tolkien, 106
Sense and Sensibility, 170, 171, 172, 173, 175
sentimentality, 44, 119
service to others, 22, 122, 186
sex, 41
in art, 60
sexual immorality, 174, 178
Shakespeare, William, 36, 147–68, 191–92
as artisan, 34, 35, 62
career in theater, 150–51
humility of, 23
personal life, 149–50
as playwright, 153–56
productions of, 148–49
tragedies of, 58
Shapiro, James, 153
Sibelius, Jean, 41
Sidney, Philip, 26
Silverstone, Alicia, 170
sin, 59, 161–66
Sindarin (elvish language), 111, 115
singing, 65
Sir Gawain and the Green Knight (poem), 110
situation comedy, of Jane Austen, 177
Snape, Severus (character), 141
snobbery, 64, 65, 177, 184
Song of Songs, 41, 60
Sophocles, 157

Spenser, Edmund, 91
spirituality, as anti-creation, 17–18
Stalin, Joseph, 147
standards, for art, 42, 53
standards of quality, as objective, 65
stewardship, of gifts, 56, 66
Stoics, 76–77
storytelling, 113
Stratton-Porter, Gene, 44–45
Strauss, Johann, 35
Stubbs, Imogen, 149
sub-creators, 19–22, 26–27, 57

tabernacle, 47, 52
Tamar, rape of, 40, 43
taste, 64, 65
technical excellence, in art, 61–62
temple, 47, 52
temptation, of power, 121
theism, Lewis on, 91
Thompson, Emma, 170
Tiamat, 80
Tiananmen Square, 73
Tolkien, J. R. R., 105–24
    chosen as greatest author of
        twentieth century, 36, 113
    on fairy stories, 81
    on giftedness, 66
    humanists on, 117
    on myths, 93–95, 107–8
    new languages of, 111–12
    as sub-creator, 26–27
    writing as gift to Christ, 106–7
Toulouse-Lautrec, Henri de, 35
traditions, respect for, 57
treasure, 138, 140, 145
tree of life, 47

truth, 62, 144
    in art, 45, 57–59
    in stories, 81, 97–98, 107, 118

unbelief, 58
unbelievers, creativity of, 32
unseen world, 106

van Gogh, Vincent, 27
Vaughan Williams, Ralph, 41
violence, 59
visualizing Christ, 48–50
Voldemort (character), 139–44

Wagner, Richard, 88–89, 95
Wakefield, Charity, 172
White Witch (character), 100–101
Winslet, Kate, 170
witchcraft
    in Harry Potter series, 126, 127,
        135, 144
    in *Macbeth*, 156–59
Woolf, Virginia, 36, 113, 173
words, 110, 113
Wordsworth, William, 88
workmanship, 62
worldliness, 37
worldview, of Shakespeare, 147,
    155–56, 157
World War I, 115
World War II, 115
worship, 46, 49, 50
writing, 113–14
    Lewis on, 97–98

Zeus, 76–77, 80

Scripture Index

Genesis
1   16, 19
1:4   16
1:10   16
1:12   16
1:18   16
1:21   16
1:25   16
1:26–28   20
1:31   16
2:18   29
3   82
3:15   81
9:8–17   19

Judges
19   40

2 Samuel
13   40

1 Kings
5   32

Job
1:6–12   82
2:1–6   82
38–41   12

Psalms
2:9   80
8   32, 70
8:1   12
8:1–3   15–16
8:3–4   20
8:5–6   20

11:4   69
19   12, 91
19:1   12
19:1–4   68
74:13–14   82, 83
104   19, 71
104:2   68
104:2–4   69
104:14–15   71
145   19, 71
145:9   71
145:14   71
148   12

Proverbs
book of   41
8   41
8:1–4   32
8:15–16   32

Ecclesiastes
book of   40
3:11   88

Song of Solomon
book of   40

Isaiah
8:1–4   51
20:1–6   51
27:1   82, 83
51:9–10   83
59:2   162

Jeremiah
13:1–11   51

16:1–9   51
18:1–11   51
19:1–13   51
51:34   83

Ezekiel
4:1–17   51
5:1–4   51
29:4–5   83
32:3–8   83

Micah
6:8   66

Zechariah
3:1–2   82

Matthew
5:5   122
5:43–48   32
5:44–45   72
6:26–29   19, 71, 72
10:29–31   19

Luke
6:35–36   72

Acts
13   76
13:22   44
14:15–17   72
14:17   32, 78
17:22–31   76
17:24–29   73–74
17:26   75
17:28   76

Romans
1   70
1:18–23   70–71
1:25   70–71
2   70

8:18–25   19
12:1–2   132

1 Corinthians
10:33   24
13   186
15   19

2 Corinthians
2:16   24
3:18   24
4:2   63
4:6   24
5:1–5   19
5:4   19
10:4–5   132

Galatians
4:19   24

Ephesians
5   188

Philippians
4:8   132

1 Thessalonians
1:6   24
5:19   132
5:20–22   53

1 Timothy
4:1–5   17, 19

Titus
1:12   76

Hebrews
11:3   13, 69

James
3:9–10   32

2 Peter
3:13   19

1 John
1:1–3   49–50
4:7–12   29n5

Revelation
4:11   12
12   79, 81, 82, 83
12:1–6   79
12:7–10   79
12:9   82, 84
12:13–17   79
21:1–4   19
21:24–26   21

What does Jesus teach us about evangelism?

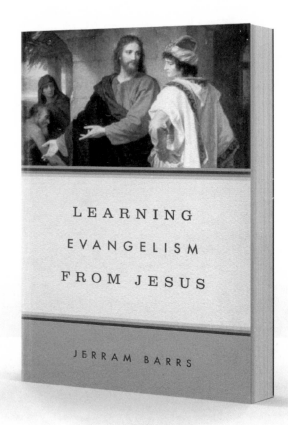

Studying Jesus's conversations with diverse people in his day, Jerram Barrs draws lessons and principles for communicating the gospel to unbelievers.

What is God's perspective on women in the Bible?

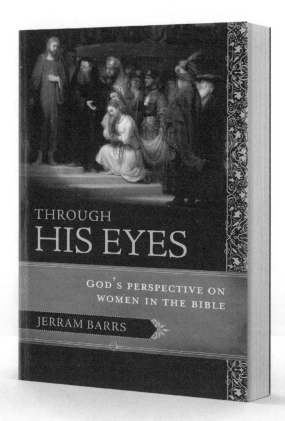

THROUGH
HIS EYES

GOD'S PERSPECTIVE ON
WOMEN IN THE BIBLE

JERRAM BARRS

Few topics have been so misunderstood as the Bible's instruction concerning women. *Through His Eyes* teaches us what God really thinks about women, how he treats them, and more.

How do we lovingly lead people to Jesus?

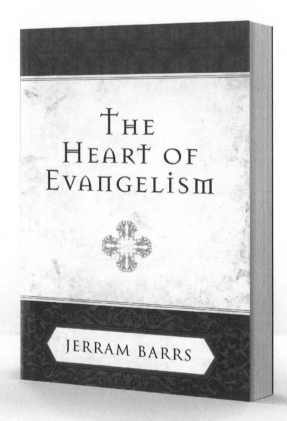

This study of evangelism graciously reminds us that the biblical model of witnessing is not one-size-fits-all. With wisdom and compassion, Jerram Barrs shows us the variety of approaches used in the New Testament to share the same true, timeless, unchanging gospel to an ever-changing audience.